# Emotional Intelligence and
# Enterprise Handbook

Also available from Network Continuum
*Future Directions* – Diane Carrington and Helen Whitten
*7 Successful Strategies to Promote Emotional Intelligence in the Classroom* – Marziyah Panju
*Pocket PAL: Emotional Intelligence* – Steve Bowkett
*Personalizing Learning: Transforming education for every child* – John West-Burnham and Max Coates

Available on Continuum
*Developing Children's Emotional Intelligence* – Helen Maffini and Shahnaz Bahman
*100 Ideas for Teaching Citizenship* – Ian Davies
*100 Ideas for Teaching Knowledge and Understanding of the World* – Alan Thwaites

# Emotional Intelligence and Enterprise Handbook

Tools and techniques to help students succeed in life and work

Cheryl Buggy

network
continuum

**Continuum International Publishing Group**
Network Continuum
The Tower Building        80 Maiden Lane, Suite 704
11 York Road            New York,
SE1 7NX               NY 10038

www.networkcontinuum.co.uk
www.continuumbooks.com

**British Library Cataloguing-in-Publication Data**
A catalogue record for this book is available from the British Library.

ISBN: 9781855394582 (paperback)

**Library of Congress Cataloguing-in-Publication Data**
A catalog record for this book is available from the Library of Congress.

Illustrations by Kerry Ingham

Typeset by YHT Ltd, London
Printed and bound in Great Britain by Cromwell Press, Trowbridge

# Contents

# Introduction

Imagine a situation where all the students in your school or college walk out of the gates for the very last time feeling enthused, positive, focused and ready and able to take the next steps in their lives. Under one arm they would have the appropriate qualifications that best suit them, be it academic or vocational, and under the other, an understanding of themselves, their dreams and aspirations and a knowledge of how to make the best of their unique potential.

There is a saying, 'boats are safe in harbour, but that's not what boats are made for'. It seems to me, not all, of course, but far too many young people find themselves tied up and leaning against the 'dockside' unmotivated, directionless and lacking in the competencies that would help them take off for the open sea and adventure. And then, even for those who do find themselves heading out to sea, there can still be problems ranging from no metaphorical chart or North Star to follow to limiting fears and lack of self belief. How many find themselves drifting with the tide, into any job, unsure of what they want from their careers or how to find it, or putting up with positions that crush their hopes and dreams.

We all suffer if we end up producing young people who become takers not givers, helpless not empowered and wasting their potential. If we could improve they way the citizens and employees of the future saw themselves, believed in themselves, were able to make good, positive, appropriate choices for their working lives and make the most of their dreams and talents, think of the benefits for all of us.

It is true that this is a handbook which, in part, is responding to the concerns and needs expressed by government and business. They worry about such things as: skills shortages, lack of employability, 'soft' skills and increasingly a need to remain economically competitive, being able to continue being inventive and enterprising. However, the handbook is primarily driven by my desire, as a teacher and a mother, to counter what I see as a terrible waste of some of the enormous potential that I see in so many of the young people I meet.

There is another saying that hits home for me and which has given rise to this handbook. It goes, 'you don't know what you don't know'. We can't blame somebody if the choices they are making are based on scant knowledge. I so often meet delegates on my training courses in the corporate world, who say they wished somebody had told them about such things as emotional intelligence when they were at school, it would have made such a difference to the decisions they made.

In essence then, this handbook has been designed to help young people become more employable and successful in their working lives, and more able to tap into their potential. It does that through the vehicles of emotional intelligence and enterprise.

As described above, this is in part because of the needs of employers. There are huge challenges facing business today, more so than ever before: the pace of change, the speed of developing technologies, the incredible rise in economic might of countries such as India and China, the need to continually innovate and be creative and enterprising. Whilst this might seem a million miles away from the business of the school day and the curriculum, I feel that we as educators owe it to our students to help them reach beyond the need to succeed academically, to the ability to develop the other skills they will need as the employees, and employers, of the future.

So what is it that the employers of today are looking for when they consider taking on a young person? They cite the following as being the desirable qualities and attributes that will help their business thrive:

- good communicator
- team player
- determined and persistent
- helpful and polite
- able to tackle problems
- positive
- proactive

- hard working and motivated
- creative and enterprising

Coincidently these desired qualities are also echoed in the emotional intelligence competencies as researched by the likes of Daniel Goleman. Goleman explored what made for excellence in the workplace. Who were the top employees and leaders and why? His list of qualities includes:

- self-awareness
- understanding and managing one's emotional state
- optimistic
- motivated
- persistent
- empathetic

There are now also a whole host of key government agendas that require teachers to focus on a combination of meeting the needs of business and developing and improving the emotional literacy and enterprise capabilities of young people. For example, in the UK the 'Every Child Matters' agenda means schools have to focus on helping students become empowered to:

- engage in decision making
- eeal with significant life changes
- be healthy and self confident
- exhibit positive behaviours
- focus on their personal and social development
- have positive relationships

# How the handbook works

The handbook is divided in the following way:

## The themes:

- me  smart

- *people* smart

- **job** smart

- future smart

Each theme is made up of a number of sessions and topics that take students on a self-developmental journey towards the world of work. The EI and enterprise competencies covered are listed at the beginning of each session and integrated throughout the entire programme.

Although each session is self contained the programme has been designed as a journey, so is best used as a continuum, with the exception of 'Job Smart'. If you are working with students under 15, you might feel it appropriate to leave this section out.

The handbook contains all the topic handouts, each made up of five points called Five things to remember, which summarize the topic. These can be copied for the students. After each topic sheet, there are suggestions on how you can deliver the topic.

At the back of the book there are supplementary activities. These have been designed to further embed the knowledge the students have gained from the programme, and to provide some practical projects and creative tasks to help them become better EI and enterprise 'practitioners'. There is also a self-assessment sheet for students which can be used after every session.

## Using guests

You might want to enhance the sessions by inviting guests to come along and share their experiences and give advice.

Below are some guidelines to help you.

## Guests are used to:

- reinforce the message or messages of the session
- add to it, by contributing their own knowledge
- share their personal stories and experiences
- join in role play activities
- take part in small group discussions
- have fun!

## Desired qualities in guests:

- able to relate to students
- good communicators
- open and prepared to share their own stories
- able to contribute in order to reinforce the 'message' of the session
- happy to talk to the whole group and work with small groups and individuals
- give their time free of charge
- able to be adaptable and flexible to the needs of the session

### Note

It is not so much what guests do necessarily, but their attitude and experiences of the world of work that counts. They need to come from as wide a range of careers and ages as possible, and a similarly wide span of academic background and ethnic mix.

## Briefing guests

The key to using guests well and maximizing their time with the students is to brief them as thoroughly as you can. This includes:

- The programme overview, and a breakdown of the sessions
- What stage the students are at in the programme
- The age and any other details about the students that may be appropriate
- The specific purpose of the session they are involved in, which includes copies of the handouts

- Ask if they have any material or advice they would like to add to reinforce or substantiate the information being given
- Describe how you would like to use them, for example, in an informal interview with you in front of the students, to be drawn in via questions relevant to the session, to join in role play or work with small groups as they tackle set activities, to feel free to add at any point to the session
- Send the list below of the sorts of questions you might ask them
- Ask them for any written information about them that will aid you in your introduction

## Potential questions for interviews with guests

- Did you have a strong sense of direction and purpose from an early age? If so, where did it come from in terms of the strongest influences in your life?
- What were your experiences of school?
- Who, or what, helped you on your way, how were they important to you?
- What do you wish you had done at an earlier age, if anything, and why?
- What knowledge would have helped you?
- What would your advice be or what useful tips would you offer on (a) your area of expertise and (b) how to get on in life and be happy?
- How essentially different is the workplace and society now, from your earliest memories? Do you need different skills or a different attitude?
- What do you think is the key to success? What does success mean to you? How do you define it?
- How do you keep balance in your life?
- What is the key to getting on with people, and how important is it?
- How do you keep yourself fit, both mentally and physically, and deal with stress?
- What is the single most important lesson you have learn in life?
- Do you have any useful advice on how to go about getting a job?
- How important is goal setting, and having a dream to pursue?
- Could you give a brief summary of your working life so far, in terms of what you do and how you got your first, and subsequent, jobs?

# Emotional intelligence and enterprise competencies

The handbook is underpinned by comprehensive research into many areas beyond that of education and business, including the fields of neuroscience, psychology and personal development. The results have been distilled and developed into the following list of six emotional intelligence and six enterprise competencies, and together these 12 competencies create the basis for the sessions and projects that follow.

**Emotional Intelligence Competencies**

 **Self-awareness**

Having a good understanding of yourself and what makes you tick.

 **Self-responsibility**

Taking ownership of your thoughts and actions. Taking responsibility for your emotional states and dealing with your feelings in a constructive and responsible way.

 **Positive and appreciative**

Having an approach to yourself and life that is constructive, helpful and optimistic. Happy to celebrate all the good things in your life no matter how small, including your skills and talents.

 **Empathetic and respectful**

Making a real effort to try to understand how somebody else might be feeling or what they might be thinking. Honouring yourself and acknowledging that everybody has a right to their opinion even if you don't agree with them.

 **Motivated**

Being driven and inspired inside yourself to achieve a set goal or goals.

 **Persistent**

Not giving up, working hard to achieve what you want to achieve. Being able to bounce back from any setbacks.

## Enterprise competencies

**Using initiative**

Taking a proactive approach to your life. Not sitting back and expecting things to just happen or be done for you by others. Anticipating and acting off your own back.

**Dealing with uncertainty**

Able to be OK with not knowing what might happen, and being able to deal with changes in a positive way.

**Creative**

Using the power of your amazing mind to make the most of your abilities, generate new ideas, solve problems and seize any opportunities.

**Courageous**

Not being afraid to take risks, being assertive and going for what you want.

**Confident**

Having healthy self belief, especially when finding yourself in new situations or meeting new people.

**Curious**

Always interested in the world around you, as well as interested in understanding yourself. Constantly asking the Why? How? What if? type questions.

For those who embrace and develop the competencies, there are many advantages.

 # Self-awareness

- you understand yourself
- it helps stop you being reactive and a victim of others
- you know what you like and what you want in life
- you can achieve your goals
- you can live by your values

- you can appreciate your strengths and work on your weaknesses.
- you communicate more effectively

 ## Self-responsibility

- you are in the driving seat of your life
- you can make things happen
- you can achieve things
- you manage your feelings
- you have better relationships with others
- you are not a victim of stress
- you keep a clear head because you do not emotionally react to the situations you find yourself in
- you are healthier and happier
- you look after yourself in the times when you are feeling hurt or upset
- you use the energy of strong emotions such as anger in a positive way
- you do not give in to your fears
- you are more in control of yourself and therefore your life

 ## Positive and appreciative

- you are happier
- you get things done and achieve more
- you are popular
- you see the good things in life and therefore value it
- you appreciate the present moment more
- you look forward to your future
- you are not put off by setbacks or your fears
- you get more out of your experiences
- you feel more positive
- you pay compliments and enjoy other people more
- you feel grateful

**Empathetic and respectful**

- you have a deeper and more meaningful understanding of others
- you react less
- you are not a victim of the words and actions of others
- you have better relationships
- people open up to you
- you are a better listener and therefore you learn more
- you avoid the need to prove yourself right
- you keep in control of your emotions when you feel strongly about something somebody has said
- you feed your self esteem and confidence
- others respond by respecting you

 **Motivated**

- you feel inspired to achieve
- you get things done
- you move towards your goals and dreams
- you overcome setbacks
- you feel energized
- you can inspire and motivate others

 **Persistent**

- you bounce back from setbacks
- you just don't give up
- you get things done
- you have a sense of achievement and satisfaction
- you learn from your mistakes

 **Using initiative**

- helps you become more creative
- you contribute to getting results for yourself and others

- makes you feel good
- adds to your sense of independence
- you can make things happen in your life
- you can help shape your own reality
- gives you energy and drive
- helps you achieve your goals
- you can get ahead

 ## Dealing with uncertainty

- you conquer your fears
- you keep a clear head and are not overcome by anxiety
- you seek and find new opportunities
- you create new opportunities
- you learn and grow
- you get more experience
- you build your confidence
- you feel more in control of you destiny

 ## Creative

- you get things done
- you come up with new ideas
- you feel excited by your thoughts
- you seize opportunities
- you develop your potential
- you innovate

 ## Courageous

- you take risks
- you achieve things
- you overcome your fears
- you feed your confidence and self esteem

- you explore new things
- you learn more

 **Confident**

- you feel comfortable in your own skin and like yourself
- you have the courage to try new things
- you challenge people and situations that you feel strongly about
- you are not likely to be bullied
- you do not worry too much about being liked because you like yourself
- you believe in yourself

 **Curious**

- you learn more about people and the world you live in
- you keep an active mind
- you can become more creative
- you make better informed decisions
- you can achieve more
- you use more of your brain's potential

## Session 1

### Aim

The aim of this session is to encourage the students to begin to explore the ingredients that make them what they are. It looks at the issues of nature and nurture, and the consequences of learned behaviour. This leads on to the subject of how the brain works and how thoughts are produced. It concludes by considering the consequences of being a negative or positive thinker.

### Materials

Three handouts: Why you are the way you are; Your amazing brain; Thinking power.
Flip chart and pens.
Room with space for group discussions.

### What happens?

Presentation by teacher/facilitator to instigate discussions, group work, individual work and concluding discussion.

As this is the very first session for the students, it is important to 'sell' them the programme by letting them know what the course can do for them, if they are prepared to keep an open mind and give the information and activities a real chance. All the knowledge in this handbook has been tried and tested by thousands of people worldwide. The issues the course addresses will be of very real value to them, now and in the future. They can begin to apply it from this very moment, and notice the difference it makes.

## EI and enterprise competencies covered:

Self-awareness, self-responsibility, confidence, positive and appreciative, motivated, creative, curious.

# Topic 1: Why you are the way you are

'Experience is not what happens to you, it is what you do with what happens to you.'

Aldous Huxley

1. **Your view of the world is shaped by the way you think and feel, and by the beliefs and attitudes you hold** ... and these in turn have been moulded by your past experiences. Most of your thinking and behaviours have been learned, and most of them have been learned in childhood.

2. **Your childhood experiences affect your adult behaviour** ... and the lessons you learn when young can become so ingrained that they can be very difficult to change the older you get.

3. **Negative conditioning can be like carrying a ball and chain around. Positive conditioning can be like a springboard to success** ... Conditioning is how your behaviour and beliefs have been shaped. Positive conditioning leaves you feeling valued, respected and loved, which in turn helps you develop a good self-image, and builds confidence. Negative conditioning can have the reverse effect.

4. **Because of the way you think, you will act in a way that will confirm your beliefs** ... and so habits are formed. Generally you will carry on with those habits for the rest of your life. For example, if you believe that you are not good at something, or not worthy, or can't be successful, that is how you will behave and what life will often reflect back to you.

5. *Here's good news!* **Although it may be tough to do, you can break old negative habits and beliefs. If you can learn something you can unlearn it. Little by little you can chip away at it until it disappears. You can then replace it with a positive, more constructive belief and thus a new habit.**

EMOTIONAL INTELLIGENCE AND ENTERPRISE HANDBOOK **15**
© CHERYL BUGGY (CONTINUUM 2008)

# Topic 1: Why you are the way you are

## TOPIC IN ACTION

Explain what conditioning is and the power it has over each and every individual's view of themselves and their world. We are a mixture of nature (born with) and nurture (taught or learned behaviours), and there is still much debate over the two and the impact they have on us. Over time we develop ways of thinking and acting that become habits which means that we do or think them automatically.

Ask the students what sorts of traits might be covered by nature (genetically inherited predispositions in terms of looks, health, possibly talents, etc.).

Introduce the concept of positive and negative conditioning, and show that these patterns of belief and behaviour begin at a very early age and vary according to our experiences.

Ask them who or what is instrumental in forming such beliefs (parents, siblings, peer group, school, society, media).

## ACTIVITY 1

Divide them into groups of four or five with a large sheet of flip chart paper and get them to brainstorm the sorts of views, opinions and behaviours that people can be taught or conditioned into believing by (a) family (b) peer group (c) school (d) society.

After five to ten minutes reassemble the groups and get each to present their findings. These can be pinned up.

Now use the points that have been raised to discuss which ones are negative, which ones positive and which ones may be neutral. In other words, which of the points serve a potentially helpful or unhelpful purpose in their lives?

Most habits are learned, and what you learn you can unlearn with practice. It might not be easy, but ask the students to reflect on the purpose of a belief that is destructive and inhibits their potential to be successful.

## ACTIVITY 2

Get them back into their original groups. Give out newspapers and ask them to go through counting the positive and negative stories. Ask them to consider the messages the paper is giving them about the world they live in. Or use magazines focusing on the adverts and the messages they carry that aim to influence the way the reader feels about themselves or their world.

Feedback results to the whole group, and discuss outcomes.

If thoughts become beliefs and habits, it's now time to explain how to break a habit that you no longer want to have. Here are some suggestions:

- admit to and own the habit
- try to understand where it has come from
- formulate a plan of what you are going to do, step by step
- get support from the right people (i.e. positive and supportive)
- practise the new way
- celebrate every positive step you take
- if you slip back, just try again and don't give up

# Topic 2: Your amazing brain

'Your brain is like a sleeping giant.'

Anthony Robbins

1. **Your brain is huge with amazing capabilities** ... You have billions of brain cells that you can use throughout your life and you will never use them all up. In fact, your brain is more powerful than any computer yet invented. Research shows that most people only use about 5 per cent of their brain's capability in their lifetime, so most of it goes to waste.

2. **Everybody is intelligent** ... and we are all intelligent in different ways. For example, some are good at maths, some at sport, some at making things, some at friendships. The term used for this is multiple intelligence and no one sort of intelligence is better than another. We also have a preferred way of taking in information.

3. **Your brain is incredibly complex and made up of sections, and each section has different functions** ... For example, when you hear a song, one part of your brain registers the tune while another part takes in the words, yet another part responds emotionally and yet another part remembers it.

4. **Your brain works more effectively if you respect your body** ... That means getting a good night's sleep, taking time to relax, eating healthy food, drinking plenty of water and exercising. Your brain is also like a muscle so if you don't use it you lose it!

5. **You can easily use more of your brain cells and therefore become smarter** ... To help you do this you need to be curious, use your imagination and be interested and focused on what you are learning. It also helps if you feel positive and confident about yourself and can see the benefits in what you are doing. That's called WIIFM? – what's in it for me?

# Topic 2: Your amazing brain

## TOPIC IN ACTION

The brain is a thing of awesome capabilities, and in most people it is dramatically underused. Its complexity is still little understood even by neuroscientists, but what we do know is that it is a bit like a muscle if you don't use it you lose it!

There are many reasons why people don't make use of their billions of neurons, for example – they might think they are not very clever, lack confidence, display lack of effort, not know how best to learn and remember or not be turned on by lessons in school.

You can never stress too many times that everybody is intelligent, everybody has an amazing brain, and we have preferred methods of taking in new information. There are three preferred learning styles – Auditory (learns best by hearing), Visual (learns best by seeing) and Kinaesthetic (learns best by doing). Most people prefer one but some are strong in two or all three.

There are currently nine recognized types of intelligence:

- bodily/kinaesthetic (sportspeople are strong in this intelligence)
- mathematical/logical
- naturalistic (attuned to and in touch with nature, for example Australian Aborigines)
- musical/rhythmic
- verbal/linguistic
- visual/spatial (pilots will be strong in this intelligence)
- existential (spiritual with a sense of being part of the universe)
- interpersonal (good at understanding others)
- intrapersonal (strong in self-awareness)

## ACTIVITY 1

Show the list of learning styles and multiple intelligences and explain them. See if the students can decide which ones suit their type/s of intelligence.

Then show them how to tap into their memory and learn some new facts by teaching them how to count from one to ten in Japanese, using the vehicle of a story. The numbers are (itchi, nee, san, she, go, roku, nana, hatchi, qu, ju). You simply take each one of the numbers in sequence, and using word association make up a story. The more crazy and funny and dramatic the tale you tell, the easier it is to remember.

For example, you have an itchy knee (itchi, nee) which you begin to scratch. You tear your trousers and sand (san) begins to pour out. Suddenly there is a crashing sound as through the window comes a flying sheep, (she) with a goat (go) holding on to it, sitting astride a rocket (roku). They land on the floor, slip on a banana (nana) skin, and hurtle towards a pile of hatching (hatchi) chicks. Just in time the chicks form a little queue (qu) and head for a nearby drink of juice (ju).

Tell the story as if it is happening in the room you are in. In that way you are taking them on a visual journey with the Japanese words.

Whilst it is a silly story the students will remember it, especially if repeated a few times. Suddenly they have very easily learned new information in a fun way. It opens their eyes to possibilities. Such storytelling and placing things around a room is the basic way world memory champions learn copious amounts of information.

Explain the power of imagination, making links, painting pictures, repetition, coming up with crazy ideas and having fun when taking in new information. It's how the brain likes to work.

# Topic 3: Thinking power

'We are what we think. All that we are arises with our thoughts. With our thoughts we make our world.'

Buddha

1. **You are constantly producing thoughts** ... In fact you produce around 50,000 thoughts a day, many of which lead to some sort of action or feeling. In fact there cannot be an action or feeling without there first being a thought.

2. **Your responses to life are shaped by your thoughts, so it's a good idea to try to be as much in control of them as possible** ... You do that by understanding why you are thinking in a particular way, and deciding consciously to change that thought if you see that it's not helpful and not in your best interests. That in turn will lead to a different feeling and a different response.

3. **You become what you think about** ... so if you choose to view yourself and the world in a positive way that is how it will generally turn out. Positive thinkers are positive people and generally experience the world in a positive way.

4. **Every thought is influenced by your memories of past experiences stored in your unconscious mind** ... so your thoughts chatter away in your head, analysing and confirming in an endless internal conversation. The unconscious mind doesn't judge and happily provides us with any useful data it has stored away to confirm a negative or a positive point of view.

5. **You can change the way you think** ... I will say it again because it is so important – YOU CAN CHANGE THE WAY YOU THINK. In changing the way you think, you can transform your life.

# Topic 3: Thinking power

## TOPIC IN ACTION

The key message of this topic is that there cannot be an action without there first having been a thought. We are constantly producing thoughts, and it is the nature of those thoughts that create our feelings, moods and actions. There is a constant conversation going on in our heads between our conscious and unconscious mind, and that conversation shapes our lives.

We are caught up in a constant loop. On top, like the tip of an iceberg, is how we behave. Under the surface is how we think, which in turn triggers feelings which leads on to a physiological response. So on it goes: Thought, feeling, reaction; thought, feeling, reaction. The skill is to break into the loop in any way possible in order to change behaviour. So you can change your thoughts, deal with your feelings and find ways to deal with such things as tension and fear for example, by taking deep breaths and shaking loose any tense muscles.

Use the handout to present these messages, focusing particularly on the vicious circle we can create – we have a negative thought, which is fed and enlarged by our unconscious mind. Before we know it our mood has changed and we experience a reality shift. As our perception of reality changes, so does what we see. It's as if our glasses prescription has changed, and lo and behold, we see the world in a different way. If we continue to focus on something, for example feeling upset, seeing the bad qualities in a person, we give it energy and so we magnify and extend that feeling.

I appreciate this is a complex issue but it is very significant. Our thoughts become our beliefs, which in turn shape our reality and therefore our lives.

The power of our thoughts is tremendous; we can literally paint pictures, and feel strong feelings, just by a thought. What is crucially important is that we can exercise some control over our thoughts, and change them if they are not helpful to us. To demonstrate the power of a thought, get the students to close their eyes and imagine a lemon sliced in half, as vividly as they can. See how many mouths begin to water! Just the mental picture is enough to trigger a physiological reaction in the body as it releases enzymes into the mouth.

To make changes in the way we think is not easy, so it is important to encourage the students to at least try. It is best to do this in easy steps by way of an experiment. To do that get them to imagine and focus on something that makes them feel good, happy, excited, and observe what happens to their feelings. To help in this activity, students could look at a picture, or play a piece of music to help trigger a feeling.

*Encourage them to listen to their thoughts and observe what is happening with them. They can then select a thought that they feel is negative and counter-productive to them, and begin the process of changing it, just like you do with any habit you are trying to break.

## ACTIVITY 1

Read out list of words and get them to write down the first thing that comes into their heads when they hear each one. For example holiday, policeman, chocolate, examinations, television, love, dark, work, politics and so on. Use any words that the students can in some way relate to, or have a reaction to.

Then, in pairs, get them to analyse where those responses might have originated, and acknowledge how quickly they produced them. Get them to examine whether the responses are negative or positive or neutral. Do the words evoke any emotional response?

How could they change a negative to a more positive response (this is called reframing).

## ACTIVITY 2

Ask them to visualize and then describe what their perfect day would be like five years from now. Encourage them to describe it in as much detail as they can, involving all of their senses, including how they feel. They must not allow a negative thought to intrude; a magic wand has been waved so that anything is possible with the exception of winning the lottery! (The perfect day activity can be used again as part of the handout Achieving hopes, dreams and goals, Topic 27.)

Stress that if this is their dream, then the programme will help them find ways to achieve it. Explore what they have learned already that could help?

## TECHNIQUE

## How to be more positive

### Recognize negative talk

Trying to change is tough. Inwardly, talk back to the negative self-talk and ask it to go away. Say STOP!

Try to avoid seeing something not working as failure. Try to see it as a result you did not want. Avoid any win/lose mindset. Be aware of the words you use to others.

Take responsibility for yourself. No one can make you feel anything without your consent. Be in charge.

Be aware of how many ways you 'programme' your brain through:

- body language
- tone of voice
- self talk
- imagination
- sounds and music
- feelings, etc.
- the words you say to others

You can control the 'software' in your brain – it is not easy, but it can be done.

Know your goals. What would you like to achieve? Be as specific as you can about what, when, where, with whom and then plan precise steps towards attaining the goal. Have a vision or dream but know you can change what you want at any time.

Ask questions of others as people like to help and give advice. Show interest in others because it builds knowledge and increases the respect others have for you. This in turn feeds your self-respect, confidence and esteem, and is a self-perpetuating process.

Prepare for positive outcomes, because expecting the best can be a self-fulfilling prophecy.

Think of 'moving towards', not 'avoidance', strategies. Focus on what is of value rather than disadvantages and disappointments. Flip the coin over – there is always an equally true motivating story for every negative limiting one.

Look at the lives of very successful individuals: what strategies did they use? Was it natural talent or hard work and perseverance, or a combination? Remember – we all have talent.

Conclude by asking if there are any questions, and round off the session with a recap of the key points from all three topics. This should include key actions: claim responsibility for your thoughts – take control – begin the change – keep trying.

### Aim

The aim of this session is to continue self-exploration. Having looked in the first session at the roots of conditioning and the origin of thoughts, the students now look at ways of tackling obstacles that can hamper, if not halt, their full development. Facing your fears, knowing who you are and what you want and having a positive outlook are all keys to becoming more emotionally intelligent and enterprising. This is what this session puts its focus on.

### Materials

Four handouts: Fear busting; Explore your uniqueness; The power of positive thinking; How to improve your self-esteem.
Flip chart and pens.
Room with space for group discussions.

### What happens?

Presentation by teacher/facilitator, discussion, group and individual work.

### EI and enterprise competencies covered:

Self-awareness, self-responsibility, positive and appreciative, courageous, dealing with uncertainty, curious, motivated, persistent.

# Topic 4: Fear busting

'Fear is that little dark room where negatives are developed.'

Michael Pritchard

1. **Fears come in all shapes and sizes and everybody is a victim of them at some time or another** ... Some fears are sensible rational ones, others are irrational and just fantasies created in our heads. Either way, it is always best to face up to your fears and reduce the power they have over you, if you can. If you don't they can keep you a prisoner and steal your enjoyment of life. As long as you are developing and learning and having new experiences fear is likely to be part of the process and that's perfectly natural.

2. **Make a list of your fears from the physical to the emotional** ... and beside each one try to establish why it is fearful to you, and see if you can trace back to where it began. This list will help you be honest and at least identify the fears that lurk in your mind. Now how about tackling one of them? To do that, ask the question below.

3. **What is the worst thing that can possibly happen?** ... Write down what the worst scenario could be. Can you deal with that as unlikely as it might be? The next thing is to ...

4. **Write down as many solutions to your fear or problem that you can think of no matter how small** ... then decide on the best solution and begin working on it immediately. Action can work wonders; it's a bit like dragging your fear into the sunshine and watching it dissolve like a vampire!

5. **Some fears are a bigger challenge than others and take longer to sort out** ... For these fears you might feel you could use professional help or the support of a reliable person you trust, because you just don't know how to deal with them. That's perfectly OK. One thing is certain, if you do not deal with fears, they do not simply go away. They can have a negative effect on your well being, and can hold you back from the success and happiness you deserve.

# Topic 4: Fear busting

## TOPIC IN ACTION

Instigate a discussion with the group to brainstorm the sorts of fears they and others experience e.g. fear of failure, rejection, change or the unknown. Share your fears with them.

Explore the difference between rational fears (sensible and useful) and irrational fears (inhibiting and often illogical).

If fears are not challenged and confronted they have a tendency to paralyse development and stop you trying something new. Fear can stop you leaving your comfort zone.

If you can, give personal examples of where you tackled and moved through that fear, in order to achieve something. Describe your feelings before and after the experience.

Get the students to remember and share fearful moments that they have experienced that turned out to be OK in the end – like the first day at secondary school, or appearing on stage or competing in a sporting event for the first time. Fears are part of life. It's our relationship with fear that is the key here. Stress that overcoming or challenging fears is such a worthwhile and liberating experience it is really worth the effort.

## ACTIVITY 1

In groups select a fear then design a fear busting poster, putting as many useful tips on it as you can.
OR
Design a short story or play for junior school children about how to face fears of moving up to senior school.

## TECHNIQUE

## Comfort zones

Draw a big circle, with a smaller one inside it so that it looks a bit like a fried egg. In the inner circle get the students to write in some of the things they are comfortable with. For example, talking to a new person, going shopping on their own. In the outer part of the circle get them to write down some of the things that that they would feel uncomfortable doing. For example, standing up and doing a presentation, moving to a new area.

The next step is to take one of those uncomfortable issues and see if, with the help of a partner, they can begin to see how they could move it into the centre by listing what action they could take or how they could reframe the way they feel about it. For example, preparing a short presentation – they could pick a topic that they know a lot about, practice in front of a friend, in front of the mirror, record it and play it back, challenge fearful thoughts, use positive self-talk and go for it!

# Topic 5: Exploring your uniqueness

'Men often become what they believe themselves to be.'

Mahatma Gandhi

1. **Spending time getting to know you is guaranteed to bring you huge pay-offs** . . . These include – a feeling of being more in control of your life, the ability to develop ways of looking after yourself in times of trouble, and a knowledge of how best you should be spending your time and developing your huge potential.

2. **So who are you?** . . . Begin by looking at your strengths and all the things you can already do. Don't be modest! Make a list of all the things you have achieved so far in life no matter how small, and list all your positive qualities. Now make a list of some of the things you are not so good at. Is there any way you can work on those by taking some action or having a more positive attitude?

3. **What values do you live by?** . . . Do you actually have a set in place? Where have they come from? Do you feel muddled and confused by the question? Then start to build a set of principles or values that you would like to live by, that can act as important guidelines and boundaries. These might include such things as – trust, honesty, openness, fun, kindness, courage and fairness.

4. **You are complex and unique with huge potential** . . . You are like a jigsaw puzzle made up of many pieces that form a picture. You can look at the various pieces and decide what you are happy with and want to keep, and what you want to change or alter, because they do not fit into the picture of who you want to be. However, if you are happy just the way you are, that's great!

5. **Self-knowledge leads to a happier you** . . . because you can build on your strengths which in turn builds self-esteem (how you value yourself). See your weaknesses for what they are, and put them in perspective. Remember you are only human and nobody is perfect, but everybody, including you, is unique and special!

# Topic 5: Explore your uniqueness

## TOPIC IN ACTION

We spend so much time learning about the world around us, but very little time really getting to know ourselves. Investing time in becoming more self-aware is really worthwhile, because it helps us to get to know what we want and why, how we are feeling, and what our strengths and weakness are. The objective is to acknowledge and enjoy the former and accept or work on the latter. Self-awareness is the cornerstone of emotional intelligence.

Read through points four and five. Self-knowledge helps you set goals and find direction in life. It also helps you own strengths and achievements, which helps build confidence and is crucial when it comes to selling yourself in an interview situation. Self-knowledge helps you to get in the driving seat of your life.

## ACTIVITY 1

Using points two and three as a guideline, divide the students into pairs. The task of each is to 'sell' the other as if they are a desirable product. This can be done in the form of an advertising poster or 60 second radio commercial. It involves listing five to ten positive adjectives that describe their qualities or personality (such as friendly, calm, loyal, caring, brave, fun, loving) or things they have achieved (such as good with computers, at sport, at driving, at cooking, at communicating).

In pairs the students then stand up and 'sell' their partner to the rest of the group. This is a very valuable activity, because it gets the students to communicate in a positive way with each other and present to the whole group. This activity often gets off to a slow start because unfortunately it is not part of everyday life to acknowledge strengths and to be paid compliments, but the end result produces a very real 'feel good' factor, especially if the lists are put up around the wall.

## ACTIVITY 2

Use point three as a focus and divide the students into two groups.

The task is to brainstorm five to ten guidelines for everyday living (this could be for school, team, family, society, group of friends). The idea of the code is to get the students to reach a consensus for harmonious living. For example (a) respect the opinions of others (b) help others wherever possible (c) accept all – regardless of creed, colour or gender (d) support for all.

Share the outcome, making the point that without a code to live by, how are you to know what is and what is not acceptable to you?

# Topic 6: The power of positive thinking

'Some people are always grumbling that roses have thorns. I am thankful that thorns have roses.'

Alphonse Karr

1. **Warning** . . . Negative thinking can seriously damage your health . . . The good news is that if you want to become more positive you can.

2. **The rewards of becoming a positive thinker are pretty impressive** . . . You are likely to become more motivated, happy, optimistic, independent, trusting, industrious, versatile, encouraging, employable and successful. Sounds good?

3. **Remember that negative thinking is learned behaviour** . . . and the way you deal with life depends on the way you think. If you are feeling negative and fearful about life it can really halt your progress, and throw a wet blanket over your ability to enjoy yourself, have fun and be successful.

4. **The first step to becoming more positive is to understand yourself** . . . Examine how you feel about yourself, and your expectations from life. If you identify a negative thought or belief, try to challenge it and make a conscious decision to reduce the power it has over you, or better still, eliminate it from your mind. Replace it with a positive one, or at the very least, a less negative one. There are times, however, when feeling negative about something that has happened to you is perfectly OK and absolutely understandable. In those situations try to find somebody you trust to help you understand and deal with how you are feeling, and be kind and gentle to yourself.

5. **Help yourself to succeed** . . . Celebrate your progress and reward yourself, set achievable goals, be gentle with yourself and expose yourself to as many good experiences as you can. Avoid, if you can, people and situations that get you down.

# Topic 6: The power of positive thinking

## TOPIC IN ACTION

We have already explored how our beliefs are shaped, and the 'selling' activity will also have brought up the fact that it's generally easier to list weaknesses and failures than strengths and achievements. Take time here, if necessary, to develop why this is the case, for example, self-effacing society, celebrity/being thin/beautiful/wealth-focused media, fear of being considered big headed or not good enough, etc.

Introduce the benefits of positive thinking, (e.g. improves confidence, motivation, assertiveness, ability to learn, determination, inspires others, makes you more employable, more successful, even more healthy).

Move through the points on the handout, sharing your experiences, and tying the information in with all that has gone before.

Remind them that positive thinking friends/employees are valuable ones!

## ACTIVITY 1

This technique demonstrates the power of the thought/feeling/reaction loop. By getting a volunteer to repeatedly use a negative phrase, the impact on their physiology becomes immediately apparent.

Get the volunteer to put up one of their arms in front of them. Tell them you want them to resist as you try to push their arm down.

Ask them to put their arm down, look you in the eye, and repeat ten times 'I am a weak and powerless person'.

Then get them to put the same arm up again to repeat the process of resistance. Their arm will go down quite easily.

Now get them to say five to ten times 'I am a strong and powerful person'. Again, repeat the attempt to push the arm down which this time will have far more power, and therefore resistance in it.

This activity demonstrates that a negative thought conveyed by the negative words 'I am a weak and powerless person', creates an almost instant physiological response. This is why successful sportspeople will tell you that their success is based on 40 per cent physical fitness and 60 per cent on having a positive mental attitude.

## ACTIVITY 2

This activity serves to show the very distinct difference between the actions and impact of negative as opposed to positive people.

Get the students into groups with a piece of flip chart paper. Ask them to design a symbol of a drain (a negative person) and a radiator (a positive person) on the paper.

Around each symbol ask them to collect the following: the words, attitudes and impact on others of these two types. For example a radiator would use words like 'can' and 'well done'. They would be helpful and positive, they would make others feel supported and encouraged.

## ACTIVITY 3

Divide the students into groups of five or so, and get them to design a feature for a magazine that targets their age group, which gives five to ten useful tips on how to get into a positive frame of mind. For example: remember a good evening out with friends that you have just had; read about somebody you admire for inspiration; buy yourself something nice; remember a time when you achieved something; remind yourself that a negative feeling can be changed; be with positive friends. Plan positive goals.

Share the outcomes with the whole group.

## ACTIVITY 4

Get the students to focus on one or two negative habits or thoughts and see if they can begin to turn them around. This is called reframing, that is, seeing the issues from a different perspective or mindset. Gradually work on eliminating such habits altogether.

## Topic 7: How to improve your self-esteem

'We ask ourselves "who am I to be brilliant, gorgeous, talented, fabulous?" Actually who are you not to be? Your playing small does not serve the world.'

Marianne Williamson

1. **Always try to see yourself in a positive light** . . . Do not put yourself down. Be aware of your strengths, acknowledge your potential, and be comfortable with the things you are not so good at. Remember, you are unique and amazing!

2. **Look after yourself** . . . Eat well, exercise, deal with stress, rest, have fun and invest in making the most of yourself.

3. **Listen to your feelings** . . . Treat them with respect, and deal with them appropriately. Don't ignore negative feelings or wait until you explode with anger, burst into tears or get really down. Take responsibility and take action.

4. **Acknowledge that you will not always get it right and will make mistakes** . . . in the way you act and feel and in the things you do. When this happens, own up, make amends or apologize. Don't beat yourself up.

5. **Be good to yourself** . . . Give yourself nurturing treats. Allow others to look after you sometimes. Don't give yourself a hard time and pat yourself on the back regularly. Try to take responsibility for your mistakes and issues without letting them get you down and depressed. Remember, we all make mistakes and nobody is perfect!

# Topic 7: How to improve your self-esteem

## TOPIC IN ACTION

From healthy self-esteem so much else flows, in terms of our attitude to, and relationship with the world at large. This session helps the students gain a fuller understanding of what is meant by the term strong self-esteem, by getting them to answer the questions in the activities below.

At the end of the session recap the following points. If you:

- understand yourself
- believe in yourself
- listen to and respect your feelings
- look after yourself mentally and physically
- be true to the things and beliefs you hold in high regard

you have many of the essential ingredients you need to become a happy and successful person, with strong self-esteem.

## ACTIVITY 1

Divide the students into small groups to discuss and come up with answers to the following:

- How would a person with high self-esteem feel about themselves?
- What would they feel about their sense of direction and purpose in life?
- Would they be positive or negative thinkers?
- What would they be like as friends?
- Would they be aggressive or assertive in the way they behaved?
- How would they deal with their emotions/thoughts/feelings?

Share outcomes with the whole group, and give real examples, if you can.

## ACTIVITY 2

Get each student to go through the handout on improving your self-esteem, and answer the following questions for themselves:

- How can you improve the way you see yourself so that it is more positive?

- How can you improve the way you look after yourself?

- What could you do that would be true to the way you want to lead your life?

- What have you done recently, no matter how small, that deserves a pat on the back?

- How could you help a friend build their self-esteem?

## Session 3

### Aim

The aim of this session is for the students to understand how communication works, and to learn and practise the valuable skill of active listening. It is also important to employers, who value staff who can get their message across in an effective and constructive way. They also value staff who, through their ability to listen well and show empathy, are strong in customer care and make good team players. From the perspective of the individual there are undoubted personal benefits to becoming an excellent speaker and listener when it comes to day to day relationships.

### Materials

Two handouts: Understanding how communication works and Active listening.
Flip chart and pens.
Spare paper.
Room with space for working in small groups.

### What happens?

Presentation by teacher/facilitator to instigate discussions, group work and concluding discussion.

## EI and enterprise competencies covered:

Self-awareness, self-responsibility, positive and appreciative, empathetic and respectful, courageous.

*people* smart

# Topic 8: Understanding how communication works

'Most conversations are simply monologues delivered in the presence of a witness.'

Margaret Miller

1. **If there is a problem, conflict, mistake or misunderstanding, it often comes down to poor communication** ... Communication is a two-way process. A message is formulated and sent, then received and interpreted. It's quite a complicated action, and there's plenty of room for misunderstanding so you can get better at it by:

2. **Improving how you send your message** ... Pick words to suit the person/s you are speaking to. Try to understand their point of view by being aware of the prejudices/mental blocks you may both have in place. Think about how they are likely to react to what you are saying. Think clearly about what message you want to get across and choose your words carefully, which includes considering their emotional impact. Make sure your words, tone of voice and body language match each other.

3. **Make sure the airwaves are as clear as possible and the time and place is right** ... Noise and interruptions can cause distractions, and it's a problem too if people are in a rush, tired, stressed or preoccupied, or if the conversation is happening in the wrong place.

4. **Listen with care** ... It's really hard work and takes a lot of concentration. When listening, we can be affected by such things as having preconceived ideas, prejudices, strong emotions, guessing what the other person is thinking or about to say and lack of attention. So, concentrate, try not to be reactive, listen to the whole message, don't interrupt, unless to ask questions to help you to understand exactly what is being said and monitor how you are feeling.

5. **Speaking well and listening effectively pays huge dividends** ... It improves relationships, allows for fewer misunderstandings and mistakes, helps build better understanding of others and saves time.

# Topic 8: Understanding how communication works

## TOPIC IN ACTION

Take the students through the communication awareness questionnaire. The purpose of the activity is to make the students further aware of the importance of effective communication in the workplace. The answers are – B,C,D,B,D,D.

## ACTIVITY 1

### Blah blah!

This activity gives the students a very real example of how 'it isn't what you say it's the way that you say it'. Using a meaningless phrase, like blah blah, over and over but putting different emotional emphases behind the words, the students can guess, usually successfully, the emotional state of the speaker. Try the emotions of enthusiasm, sadness, worry, happiness and see how well they interpret the emotions and guess correctly.

## ACTIVITY 2

Stress the point that any communication is a two-way process, and ask them how they think the process could fall down (e.g. the mood of each person, interruptions, not listening or concentrating, thinking about something else, noisy environment, preconceived ideas, prejudices, tone of voice and body language in conflict). Read through point five of the handout. Give any personal examples to add to or reinforce the message. Write their answers on the flip chart.

## ACTIVITY 3

In a role play situation, demonstrate very poor communication in action.

Suggested scenario:
A new work experience person is meeting the boss for the first time. Unfortunately the boss is stressed and bad tempered, and after a cursory introduction launches into complicated instructions to complete some urgent calls. The new person is very passive and fearful and does not understand, but does not ask for clarification. A little later the boss returns to find the job not done and gets angry.

Get the students to identify as many mistakes made by both characters as they can.

Repeat the role play, this time doing it effectively, for a win-win outcome.

## ACTIVITY 4

Divide the students into groups of four.

Set the following scenario to role play, first badly, then well. Make sure two students are observers, making notes and giving negative and positive feedback. The scenario could be a student asking for an extension on an overdue project. The teacher is busy and stressed. The projects have to be in and marked by a set date according to examination dictates, however, the student has been helping out with a family problem and has not had the time to do justice to the project. Or get them to create their own scenario.

**1.** The percentage of time the average worker spends communicating is?

    A 25%        B 40%        C 50%        D 85%

**2.** Success in business is ... % dependent on effective communication and inter-personal skills?

    A 15%        B 50%        C 85%        D 100%

**3.** The percentage of communication time spent listening is?

    A 10%        B 20%        C 33%        D 45%

**4.** The percentage of communication spent writing is?

    A 9%        B 12%        C 18%        D 25%

**5.** The percentage of workplace mistakes attributable to poor communication is?

    A 28%        B 40%        C 65%        D 70%

**6.** The percentage of a message that is communicated non-verbally is?

    A 15%        B 28%        C 55%        D 75%

© CHERYL BUGGY (CONTINUUM 2008)

- Suitability – use words that are relevant to the listener.

- Accuracy – be as specific as possible.

- Paint pictures with words – using metaphors and similes. This helps you to be more interesting and memorable.

- Be objective when imparting information – if you are biased say so.

- Use 'and' instead of 'but' – in order to value others' opinions.

- Avoid jargon – unless it's appropriate. If you must use it then explain it and why it is essential.

- Use interesting stories – as well as useful phrases and quotations.

- Use a dictionary/thesaurus to increase your vocabulary.

- Be aware of phrases where the meaning is not as it seems e.g. 'With the greatest respect', 'I hear what you are saying', 'I appreciate that but... ' In reality such statements can mean the opposite!

- Be constructive. Tell people what you want them to do rather that what you want them to avoid e.g. not 'don't ignore me when I speak to you'. Use instead 'I would really like it if you listened to me when I speak to you'.

# Topic 9: Active listening

'Drawing on my fine command of the English Language, I said nothing.'
Robert Benchley

1. **Don't talk about yourself** . . . Focus on the speaker and make encouraging noises, nod and use your face and eyes to show interest.

2. **Ask questions** . . . open and closed ones. For more information use ones that demand more than a Yes or No answer (e.g. starting with What, Why, When, Where and How). To stop the flow of the talker use closed questions (e.g. starting with Did, Do or Is).

3. **Sum up** . . . what has been said every so often to check that you have been hearing OK. You can use metaphors to do this (e.g. did it feel as though you were banging your head against a brick wall?) or similes (e.g. was it like speaking to an alien?).

4. **Check out feelings** . . . You may pick these up in the body language ('I noticed you smiled when you were talking about . . . does that mean you are pleased . . .?').

5. **Allow for silence** . . . Give people time to pause and think.

# Topic 9: Active listening

## TOPIC IN ACTION

We are never taught how to be an active listener, despite the fact that we spend nearly half our communicating time listening. Not surprisingly, we often do it badly.

All sorts of things get in the way of being an effective listener, so brainstorm with the students just what those things could be. For example:

- distractions
- thinking about what we want to say next
- making value judgements and not giving the speaker a chance
- getting overemotional and reactive
- daydreaming
- giving off conflicting body language, including eye contact
- still focused on what has happened before this conversation or what we are about to do next, i.e. not focused in the present moment

Discuss and list the positive things that come out of active listening. It:

- improves relationships
- allows for fewer misunderstandings
- helps you understand more and become less emotionally reactive
- makes you more effective in your work

Go through the handout and/or use the following.

## ACTIVITY 1

Show the mnemonic CARESS model.

Concentrate – focus only on the speaker.

Acknowledge – show your interest and attention to the speaker.
Research – ask questions, and respond well to the answers.
Exercise emotional control – stay calm and don't react or be provoked.
Sense the non-verbal message – what is the body language and tone of voice saying?
Structure – try to organize the information as you receive it.

Then get the students to do the same with the word 'Listen' or 'Communicate'.

## ACTIVITY 2

Divide the students into groups of three, each taking it in turns to be the observer, speaker or listener.

First show the students how not to do it by role playing with another student. Suggested scene: Ask the student about their journey to school today. Then show very little interest in the answers in both your body language and the fact you jump in with your own story whenever you can, or yawn, look at your watch, take a call from your mobile, etc.

Get the students to identify how you are being a poor listener. Then get them to practise active listening, with the observer giving feedback, using the tips on the handout, or the 'Caress' model. (Possible subjects could be: how are you getting on with your subjects at school; what do you do in your spare time; where did you go on your holidays; what career do you want to follow; where do you shop; what music/bands do you like?)

## ACTIVITY 3

### Van Gogh's nightmare communication activity

Get the students into pairs.
Get them to sit back to back.
One is the drawer the other the describer.
Give the describer an abstract diagram or object to describe.

The drawer has to follow the instructions and draw what their partner is describing. They cannot ask questions or turn around.

When they have finished the drawing they can show their partner what they have drawn and be allowed to see what they should have drawn to see how close they came to getting it right!

## Session 4

### Aim

The aim of this session is to build on the communication foundations of the last session. Reinforce that from a business perspective. Good communication skills are essential qualities to have in employees, both in terms of customer care, and working as an effective team player. In this session we focus on three specific skills: having courageous conversations; giving compliments; and being assertive.

### Materials

Three handouts: Giving compliments; Courageous conversations; Being assertive.
Flip chart and pens.
Room with space for group work.

### What happens?

Presentation by teacher/facilitator, group discussion and practical activities. This is the start of a series of topics that all aim to further improve how the students communicate. It gets them to explore the process, and practise using words and phrases that have been carefully considered.

## EI and enterprise competencies covered:

Self-awareness, self-responsiblility, positive and appreciative, empathetic, courageous, dealing with uncertainty, creative, confident.

# Topic 10: Giving compliments

'Wise men appreciate all men for they see the good in each.'

Baltasar Gracian

1. **Smile and look pleased** ... Compliments are a great free gift that you constantly have at your disposal. They cost nothing, and give great pleasure to the receiver as well as you, the giver. However, they must be given in a genuine way.

2. **Stick to the point** ... Don't idolize or overgeneralize. e.g. not 'You are the most wonderful person in the whole world ever', but 'Thank you so much for helping me out yesterday'.

3. **Don't add 'put-downs' of you** ... e.g. 'You look great, not a wreck like me.'

4. **Don't add a 'sting in the tail'** ... e.g. 'You've been really nice today, I wish you were always like that.'

5. **Give often** ... The more you give compliments the better you feel!

# Topic 10: Giving compliments

## TOPIC IN ACTION

The giving and receiving of compliments is an area some people seem to have difficulty with. Maybe that's because we so often focus on the negative in ourselves and others, or think how things are not as good as they could be, so that giving compliments and praise to others tend to fall by the wayside.

It is certainly true that people who are positive and confident, with healthy self-esteem regularly praise others and receive compliments gracefully.

Not only is it positive to give praise, it also makes the giver of the compliment feel good too. Therefore it's time for a little practice!

Read through the handout on giving compliments.

Encourage the students to use these compliments at some point in time and to get in the habit of giving compliments on a regular basis.

## ACTIVITY 1

Show how not to give a compliment in role play. Then demonstrate how to do it well.

Ask the students to write down a compliment they could pay to each member of their family, to all their friends and to others they are associated with, such as members of staff and others who work at their school.

Next get the students into small groups and encourage each member in turn to pay a compliment to the person beside them. This obviously works best if students know each other quite well. It can be an awkward and challenging activity but is well worth doing.

An alternative is to place a piece of A4 on the wall for each student and get everybody to write a positive comment on it. Or in a group write a compliment under somebody's name then fold the paper and pass it on. Everybody ends up with a fan of compliments which they should be encouraged to keep.

Encourage the students to pay compliments they have come up with when they leave the classroom and when they get home. Next time you see them get some feedback on how the compliments were received.

# Topic 11: Courageous conversations

'All conversations are with myself and sometimes they involve other people.'
Susan Scott

1. **Choose the right time and the right place** . . . not in front of others, not when stressed or too emotional. Plan what you are going to say beforehand.

2. **Try to start in a positive way** . . . e.g. if it's appropriate, talk about some of the good points of the other person and that you hope to have a good outcome as a result of what you are about to say.

3. **Stick to the point and be specific** . . . Give dates; times; figures; frequency. Sound confident in your words and have positive body language. If they become reactive do not do the same. Take a deep breath, keep calm and focused.

4. **Don't just blame, take some responsibility** . . . If it's appropriate, acknowledge your part. Also don't drag the opinions of others into this.

5. **Focus on what the person has done, not their personality** . . . Focus on their actions or their behaviour. Do not condemn the whole person.

# Topic 11: Courageous conversations

## TOPIC IN ACTION

The important thing to avoid in courageous conversations is to create a situation where the person being challenged becomes instantly reactive and therefore unreceptive to what is being said. So, go through the handout which simply and clearly explains how to have a constructive courageous (thereby potentially challenging) conversation.

Introduce the students to the technique below. It is an extremely effective tool when making assertive requests. It helps prepare and structure what is to be said to ensure maximum impact.

The technique is simple and powerful. It's good to learn it by heart and practice using it regularly. Preparing 'in your head' what you are going to say helps keep focus and builds confidence and a sense of control.

## TECHNIQUE

## Method:

### 1 – Explain the situation

- be brief
- be fair and objective
- keep to the point
- don't give reasons, justifications or explanations as to why you think the problem has happened

### 2 – Describe how you feel

- explain how you are feeling about the situation
- empathize with the other person's feelings to show you understand and appreciate the situation

### 3 – Describe what you need

- state your request clearly and specifically
- be realistic in what you are asking for
- offer to compromise if it feels right and you are happy to do so

### 4 – Consequences (optional)

- Finish your statement on a positive note by outlining the rewards the other person can expect from agreeing to your request. If that fails, then you might need to spell out a negative consequence.

## Technique in action

'Janet, three month ago you asked to borrow some money from me and you promised to repay me within four weeks. On three occasions I have asked you for the money and each time you have said that you will. However, you have still not done so.' (Explaining the situation.)

'I am feeling let down and pretty upset that you have not kept your promise. I do understand you have had some money worries, and that things have been difficult for you.' (Feelings with empathy statement.)

'I need you to pay me the money you owe me by the end of this week, or at the very latest, by Wednesday of the following week.' (Needs.)

'If you do that, then our friendship will not be affected, and I am sure I will be able to help you out in the future if you need me to.' (Positive consequence.)

'If you don't do as I have requested, I will find it very difficult not to get angry and that could affect our friendship.' (Negative consequence.)

## Broken record technique – (to add to the one above if required)

The broken record technique is another useful tool to use when having a courageous conversation, or in any situation where you need to keep focused. Just as a scratched record gets stuck and keeps repeating the same sound over and over again, so, when using this technique, the same statement is repeated for as long as is necessary to make the point.

## Method:

- Choose one sentence that sums up what you want.
- Repeat the sentence over and over again.
- Use a relaxed body language and calm, firm voice.
- Either ignore arguments, emotional blackmail, 'red herrings', objections, distracting questions or asides, etc., or quickly acknowledge with an empathy statement.
- The broken record phrase from the example above would be 'I need you to pay me the money by the end of the week.' So you could say for example 'I appreciate you are upset and worried about money, however, I need you to pay me the money by the end of the week.'

## ACTIVITY 1

Use both techniques in the following activity.

Examples: being badly let down by a friend; returning faulty goods to a shop; somebody using your mobile without your permission; a friend late for a night out then leaving you in the venue and going off with somebody else.

Get one student to use the technique, one to receive and respond to it and the others to give feedback and discuss how each felt about the activity.

## Topic 12: Being assertive

'The best way is always through.'

Robert Frost

1. **Be calm** ... Look and be relaxed and in control (helped by practising before-hand!) If necessary before you begin to speak or act, take some deep breaths and use your imagination to visualize a positive outcome to what is about to happen. Tell yourself mentally 'Everything will be OK.'

2. **Be direct and open** ... Speak directly to the person concerned; don't beat about the bush. Instead spell things out clearly.

3. **Be respectful** ... Be polite; listen attentively; acknowledge that everyone has a right to their own opinion.

4. **Be persistent** ... Don't take 'no' for an answer first or second time around. Stick out for what you believe is just and fair and what you want.

5. **Be courageous** ... Be prepared to take risks; admit to your faults and mistakes; give honest feedback; share your beliefs, views, ideas and feelings even though they may be dismissed or disliked. It takes courage but ask for help and support if you feel you need it.

# Topic 12: Being assertive

## TOPIC IN ACTION

This topic involves plenty of role play, so to break the ice, demonstrate how to be assertive with another person or student.

Assertiveness is often confused with aggressiveness, and although they do share some things in common they are quite different ways of behaving.

Use one or more of the following activities:

## ACTIVITY 1

Divide the students into two groups, each taking either assertiveness or aggressiveness as their subject. Find answers to the following questions to be presented to the whole group on conclusion:

- Think of 3–5 adjectives to describe the general attitude of an assertive/ aggressive person.
- Give 3–5 words or phrases they might use.
- What could their body language be like?
- What could their sense of humour be like?
- How would they drive?
- What is positive about being assertive/aggressive?
- What is negative about being assertive/aggressive?

In sharing the results of their discussions, the students should end up with a much clearer understanding of what assertiveness is, and why it is a desirable style of behaviour to adopt.

## ACTIVITY 2

The technique used in courageous conversations is also used here. It is vital to stress the need for preparation before any important communication.

Your boss has asked you to work late, without any notice, because somebody has not turned up for their shift. This is not the first time this has happened, and last time you agreed, but it meant missing your evening class. There have been job cutbacks already, so everybody at work is having to work extra hard and there is a feeling of insecurity at times. You like your job, and certainly need the money, but increasingly feel under pressure, and your boss has increased that pressure by asking you to stay. Put your point of view, applying the five points outlined on your Being Assertive handout.

## ACTIVITY 3

In groups of 2/4/6 use these case studies:

Simon worked in a night club for two hours every evening 'bottling up' and collecting glasses. His work was basic but paid him what he needed and he did a good job. One evening the cleaner has failed to turn up and the manager of the club asked Simon to 'muck in' as there was no one else to do it. Simon felt awkward saying 'No' and, although cleaning the toilets wasn't something he wanted to do, he needed to keep the job. The next night the manager asked him to do the cleaning again and explained that the cleaner had actually been sacked.

What would you suggest Simon does next? How should he behave?

## ACTIVITY 4

Sarah and John had known each other for a year and were very happy in their relationship, so they decided to find a flat and move in together. Sarah wanted to redecorate, but John didn't feel this was necessary. They had their first major argument on the day they moved in. During the first weeks, John found Sarah stubborn and controlling. She wanted the flat tidy, for John to be at home with her in the evening and for him to come to Sunday lunch with her parents every weekend. Sarah felt John was lazy and uncaring. He had changed since they had moved in together and now she wondered if they ought to end their relationship.

What do they need to do to try to sort the situation out? What advice would you give them? Script the conversation they could have that would be constructive.

## ACTIVITY 5

Get the students to select a current scenario from a soap that they watch, where there is a relationship or friendship issue. In pairs, get them to write a letter of advice to the characters describing what they could do to rectify the problems they are experiencing. A variation on this could be to resolve the situation through a class discussion or role play.

To further clarify, read through the handout Being assertive. You may wish to copy the CONFIDENCE mnemonic to give to the students.

**C**ompromise – only if it feels right to do so.
**O**pen – be honest.
**N**egotiate – but firmly.
**F**air – to yourself and others.
**I**nnovate – be creative.
**D**irect – get to the point.
**E**xpressive – say what you are feeling.
**N**on-verbal – be aware of what your body language is saying.
**C**hance – be courageous, take risks if it feels right.
**E**xpectation – visualize a positive result.

Assertiveness is usually defined by the following descriptors: Direct, respectful, fair, courageous, open, good listener, calm and confident.

## Session 5

### Aim

The focus this session is to further develop the students' communication skills as you encourage them to consider the impact their words have on others. The session then moves its focus to the importance of teamwork and working with others.

### Materials

Three handouts: Dealing with challenging people; Working with others; Winning teams.
Flip chart and pens.
Room with space for group work.

### What happens?

Continued practical activities by students, with advice from the teacher/facilitator, presentation of handout points and group discussions.

### EI and enterprise competencies covered:

Self-awareness, self-responsibility, confidence, empathetic, courageous, dealing with uncertainty, creative, using initiative, positive and appreciative, persistent.

# Topic 13: Dealing with challenging people

'Nobody can make you feel inferior without your consent.'

Eleanor Roosevelt

1. **In dealing with challenging people you are really dealing with challenging behaviour** ... So focus on the behaviour of the other person and remember what you need to be good at is knowing how to manage your side of the conversation. If at all possible, try to keep the channels of communication open, so you can work at resolving any problems, so keep talking and listening.

2. **If somebody is being rude, impatient or angry, try not to accept and react to the negatives they are throwing your way** ... Try to find out what the problem is, listen carefully and attentively, give feedback, ask questions and above all, remain calm and reasonable and don't get emotionally reactive e.g. upset, angry or defensive.

3. **Make sure you are in control of your emotions** ... and don't let others spoil your day! Of course, that is easier said than done, especially if somebody touches one of your 'sensitive spots', but surely it's better to take charge of your feelings rather than let others control them?

4. **Dealing with challenging people is much easier if you are feeling good about yourself** ... If you are coming from that confident position, you are unlikely to react in a negative way in any situation you find yourself in. It also helps if your self-esteem is healthy and you know how you expect and are prepared to be treated by others.

5. **In dealing with challenging people you are aiming to find a solution to the problem** ... Compromise if possible, but do not be reduced to a winner/loser scenario, and do not be bullied. If you feel bad afterwards it's important to speak to a supportive listener, and not ignore your feelings. It is also perfectly OK to walk away from a situation if you cannot cope with the other person's behaviour or your feelings.

# Topic 13: Dealing with challenging people

## TOPIC IN ACTION

The key point to stress in this topic is that it is the challenging behaviour that we need to tackle, not challenging people. This moves the focus to the specific behaviour that needs to be understood and dealt with.

Trying a little empathy and understanding goes a very long way, and if coupled with a determination to produce a win-win outcome can prevent a reactive argument, sense of victimhood, resentment or frustration that can happen in any difficult communication.

Go through the handout dealing with any questions, and inviting comments.

## ACTIVITY 1

Brainstorm and compile a list of the sorts of behaviour people find challenging, (e.g. aggressive, patronizing, passive, distant, too jokey, self-centered, rude, bored).

Get the students to explore how and why they react to any of the above. Can they come up with constructive ways of dealing with their reactions?

## ACTIVITY 2

Get four volunteers.

Give three a type of behaviour (passive, aggressive or assertive). The fourth is the waiter.

Set the scene. They are three friends meeting at a restaurant to plan a holiday. The service is particularly poor.

Get them to act out the scenario.

Ask the audience to guess who of the three friends is assertive, who aggressive and who passive.

## TECHNIQUE

## Control Your emotional temperature

There are times when other people's behaviour can make us angry. As soon as you feel that anger beginning inside you, the following technique is very useful.

The aim is to prevent your anger boiling over into loss of control. That does not mean that you are never allowed to be angry or express your feelings if somebody has behaved badly. What it does mean though, is that you deal with your anger in a more controlled and more effective way.

## Technique in action

As you become aware that you are getting angry you follow the steps below so that, by your actions, you trick your brain into thinking everything is OK.

### Step 1

Distance – let go of any physical contact, take a step back, lean back on a chair. Put some space between you and the other person.

### Step 2

Ground yourself – bring yourself down to earth by taking hold of something and distract yourself by mentally going through a list of things you have to do or reciting a poem or the seven times table in your head.

### Step 3

Let go of tension – clench and unclench your fists (behind your back!), or curl and uncurl your toes so that you that you consciously relax them.

## Step 4

Focus on your breathing – take some deep relaxing breaths to calm your pulse. Keep this up for a few moments.

These physical actions actually 'trick' the brain into thinking you are quite OK and keeping calm.

## ACTIVITY 3

Explore things that make the students angry, and use some of your own experiences and stories to help this, if you feel comfortable doing so. You could devise some role play scenarios to practise the technique above or get them to design a poster using a mnemonic for 'In Control'.

*people* smart

# Topic 14: Working with others

'When you handle yourself use your head; when you handle others, use your heart.'

Donna Reed

1. **Whatever you do or wherever you go you will find people** ... so regardless of what age they are, or what they do or what position they hold, treat people as people. Don't think titles think human beings! Try to respect everybody.

2. **Get to know the people you spend time with** ... and try to build good relationships. Be friendly, helpful, interested, polite, and respectful. Welcome newcomers that join your class or group or team.

3. **Treat everybody you spend time with as a 'member' of the same team** ... Find out what people's strengths are and be clear what you can offer.

4. **Always try to help** ... Never say 'it's not my problem'. It is claimed that a team or group is only as strong as its weakest member, so see how you can help any weak links.

5. **Understand the group or class or year group you are part of but don't treat it as an island** ... You work as part of a small team within a much bigger team, so try to see the big picture, and appreciate and value your part in it.

# Topic 14: Working with others

## TOPIC IN ACTION

Working with others is something all of us do every day at some level or another.

We can define 'team' as working together for a common purpose, from dealing with the small day to day issues, to the major ones.

Begin by getting the students to list what sorts of 'teams' they are in (family, friends, class, sport, band, etc.).

Being a strong team player is not only highly valued by employers, it can have enormous impact on the outcome of any task that involves a group of people. In other words one person's attitude and actions can, and do, make a difference to any outcome.

It is also important for a team to see the big picture, be it positive or negative. That means seeing beyond the immediate environment, to the whole organization and beyond. So for example in a football team, each player will work on their strengths, they will understand the way others in the team work, and they will also spend plenty of time watching their competitors in action.

Take the students through the handout.

Finish by giving personal examples of how you:

Function as part of a team in your work.

How crucial it is to do so.

How being team motivated does not mean you cannot also look out for yourself and your own fulfilment.

## ACTIVITY 1

Get the students to offer what attitudes and qualities they can bring to a team (e.g. good listener, well organized, supportive, creative, hard working, leader, helpful, focused).

*people* smart

## Topic 15: Winning teams

'Ask not what your team mates can do for you, ask what you can do for your team mates.'

Magic Johnson

1. **We are all part of teams** . . . from family and friends to work and hobbies. It's up to you to decide what part you play and what you choose to take out of the experience.

2. **Being 'me centred' does not make for a winning team** . . . Remember, no one person makes a team. You and your needs are important, but common goals and passions can bring huge rewards. Remember, none of us are as good as all of us.

3. **Be committed to your team** . . . Do not think failure, or be apathetic, or give in to fear. Instead, give your very best and believe in yourself and your team. Don't be a victim. If at times you feel you are being dumped on, remember it's how you respond that matters. Remember, together everybody achieves more.

4. **Want the best from everybody** . . . Help sustain and build self-confidence. Your attitude can make all the difference. You can really affect performance when you help others and it makes you feel good too! Remember, there is no 'I' in team.

5. **See the big picture** . . . Successful teams research and investigate their opponents or competitors. It helps overcome blockages, prepares you for the unexpected, gives you the edge, and helps challenge any fear you may have.

# Topic 15: Winning teams

## TOPIC IN ACTION

This topic further reinforces the information covered in the previous topic.

Take the students through the points, asking for feedback from any in the group who have particular experience of teamwork. Share your stories too.

## ACTIVITIES

The remaining time is for team activities.

For example, use the red/black game; air crash activity; or the tower building activity (see Supplementary activities).

After playing any of the team challenges, get them to debrief to explore how they performed. You could also appoint observers to give feedback.

## Aim

The aim of this session is to encourage the students to begin to think about how they appear to others, particularly when it comes to first impressions, and how best they can sell themselves to others. It also gives guidelines on how to begin the search for a job, which builds on earlier foundations of knowing yourself, and the importance of positive thinking. It concludes by giving tips on how the job hunting process best works.

## Materials

Four handouts: Packaging and developing your potential; Getting the job you want; Effective methods of getting a job; Improving your job hunting success.
Flip chart and pens.
Copies of current newspapers with job sections.
Room with space for group work.

## What happens?

Presentation by teacher/facilitator, individual work and group discussion.

## EI and enterprise competencies covered:

Self-awareness, self-responsibility, using initiative, motivated, creative, courageous, dealing with uncertainty, confidence, persistence, positive and appreciative, curious.

# Topic 16: Packaging and developing your potential

'A man with a good coat upon his back is more likely to be well received than he with a sloppy one.'

Samuel Johnson

1. **Making a good first impression** . . . is important and you only get one chance at it. They are made very quickly and, good or bad, have a habit of sticking.

2. **You are your greatest asset** . . . So it makes sense to dress well and make the most of yourself. Add to that good grooming and positive body language – upright, shoulders back, smile, firm handshake and good eye contact.

3. **Avoid mistakes by knowing what suits you** . . . Select the right shapes, colours and styles that are right for you and fit the impact that you want to have.

4. **Dress to impress the people who matter in your life** . . . Imagine yourself in a job or at important interviews or events. How do you want to look and what kind of impression do you want to make?

5. **Looking good helps you feel good** . . . and a positive frame of mind is more likely to bring you positive results. It also boosts your confidence and self-esteem. So invest time and energy in making yourself look good from top to toe.

# Topic 16: Packaging and developing your potential

## TOPIC IN ACTION

The essential message of this topic is the impact of first impressions and the power of non-verbal communication, not only in the interview situation, but whenever meeting anybody for the first time.

In the first 10–40 seconds of meeting 90 per cent of all people will form an opinion of you.

55 per cent is given to how you are dressed and your general grooming.

38 per cent is how you physically present yourself i.e. body language and your tone of voice.

7 per cent is what you have to say. That's all!

## ACTIVITY 1

Show students a selection of bags full of objects that have high symbolic value, in order to get them to make value judgements about the owner of the objects.

Questions to address. From the objects in front of them, they must decide the following about their imagined person:

£ What type of clothes do they wear?

£ What type of car do they drive?

£ What sort of house do they have?

£ What kinds of words (vocabulary) do they tend to use a lot?

£ What sort of job do they do?

£ How do they spend their leisure time?

£ Where would they go on holiday?

£ What is their age and name?

This is a fascinating activity. The students will have no problems building a strong stereotype of the person concerned. They will make assumptions, and draw conclusions based on their own prejudices, preconceived ideas and conditioning. In an ideal situation it would be good if you could offer a selection of bags containing objects that all belong to you, and for each bag to contain objects that show a different aspect of you and your life.

# Topic 17: Getting the job you want

'The people who get on in this world, are the people who get up and look for the circumstances they want and if they can't find them, they make them.'

George Bernard Shaw

1. **What do you want to do or be?** ... Make a list of the things you enjoy, are good at and give you satisfaction, and a list of things you hate doing, are not interested in at this moment in time, and things you feel you are not good at. Now you have a starting point.

2. **Investigate, research and explore** ... Test out your choices. Talk to people, work shadow, read relevant books and journals, try voluntary work or work experience, use the internet. As you research, ask yourself can you see yourself doing this, five days a week nine to five? Ask if you might be ruling out things, or focusing on other things for the wrong reasons. Become your own personal detective.

3. **Set some goals** ... Goals can motivate you and get you going. They can be short, medium or long term targets or even better all three! Goals help you to head in the right direction; give you drive and a sense of purpose. They can always be changed and adjusted at a later date, if necessary.

4. **Network** ... Keep your eyes and ears open, talk to anybody who might help or give advice, get to know them. Join professional organizations, associations, groups or clubs. Keep a contacts book of people and anything relating to the work you are interested in.

5. **Don't give up, persist** ... Keep positive and show willingness, be curious, versatile and flexible, try every avenue to move towards your goal, and be open to options.

EMOTIONAL INTELLIGENCE AND ENTERPRISE HANDBOOK
© CHERYL BUGGY (CONTINUUM 2008)

# Topic 17: Getting the job you want

## TOPIC IN ACTION

It is quite common for students to have very little idea about what they really want to do when they leave full time education. That's OK, except the consequences can result in some students feeling lost, demotivated, confused, making poor choices and leaving their huge potential untapped.

Others might feel that getting a good job will be difficult, that work is something to be endured not enjoyed, or, unrealistically, that they can step to the top of the ladder straight away!

Some believe that winning the lottery or seeking celebrity status is the answer to their future happiness and success.

Use point one on the handout to get the students to begin to consider the options via their likes and dislikes, bearing in mind the positive quote at the top. It may have been written a while ago but it is still true that life is largely what you make of it, and you can create your own opportunities, as well as argue for your own limitations!

## ACTIVITY 1

Get the students to make a list of the things they don't want to do, or are not any good at.

Alongside that, they can make a list of things they do want to do and are good at or would like to become good at, e.g:

| No | Yes |
|---|---|
| Same office every day 9–5 | Lots of travel, flexible hours |
| Same old faces | Meeting people |
| Not well organized | Friendly, good communicator |
| Methodical routine | Creative |
| Lots of systems and statistics | Variety |

They could also add how doing the things on the left would make them feel and do the same for the ones on the right.

## ACTIVITY 2

Get the students into groups. Give each group a piece of flip chart paper with a different career heading. Get them to see how many jobs they can come up with within three minutes then get them to pass their sheet on to the next group clockwise so that they in turn have to add to another group's list, and so on. This means they increasingly have to think out of the box, as the more obvious careers will already be on the list. You can end up, after about ten minutes, with a huge number of possible career choices. Suggested themes – working with animals, caring professions, leisure and tourism, retail. This activity serves to widen horizons and possibilities and stimulate creativity.

## ACTIVITY 3

Write in the centre of a piece of paper the job you want/sort of work you would be interested in doing. Write around that how you could find out more, for example:

TV visit/work shadow      Hospital/community radio      Careers Office

Library

Journalism

Internet

Local newspapers      School/college      Family

Newspapers      Magazines      Friends

## ACTIVITY 4

Set yourself five things you would like to achieve in:

6 months     1 year     2 years     5 years     10 years

Add to each one what you think you are going to have to do to achieve them. This could be presented in the form of a tree (with trunk, branches and leaves), ladder, (using the rungs as the steps to success) or game (e.g. golf, with each shot/hole representing a step towards the goal of success).

## ACTIVITY 5

Brainstorm, as a group, how to network. (If you need to, explain the word 'network'. You could use the analogy of a spider's web with its interconnecting strands.) The task is to find out a list of people who would be good to interview about a career of their choice. For example a job in advertising – contact local companies, do an internet search of agencies that offer advertising as a service, contact local FE and HE organizations, Chamber of Commerce, Federation of Small Businesses, Institute of Directors, any of the school governors, etc., as potential contacts to help you find out more.

## ACTIVITY 6

It could well be that some students fancy setting up their own business, and that is to be encouraged. There are many great success stories of business empires growing out of small simple ideas.

Get the students to research how a well known business started, for example, Virgin, Woolworths, Nike. Or, if they have their own business idea, describe what it is and what they will need in place to start it up and progress with it.

# Topic 18: Effective methods of getting a job

'The major difference between successful and unsuccessful job-hunters is not some factor out there, but the way they go about their job hunt.'

Richard Nelson Bolles

1. **The creative job-hunting approach** ... has an 85 per cent success rate for those who follow it thoroughly. Figure out your best skills and favourite knowledge. Research employers that interest you and contact the person who can employ you.

2. **Applying directly to an employer can also work** ... having first done your homework. Approach companies you think you might like to work for, call in and ask to see someone – the boss, if possible, and sell yourself. Ask for work shadowing opportunities, offer to help out for free for a set time. Obviously don't expect to walk in and talk to the CEO of Tesco, and you have to be prepared to cope with quite a few rejections!

3. **Ask friends and relatives for job leads** ... both are effective. The point of both of them is to get others to put out feelers for you. However, you must be specific and tell them what it is you are looking for. For example 'I am looking for some experience or opportunities working with animals', not 'I'm looking for a job'.

4. **Use the careers office at your school or college** ... They have plenty of information, advice and contacts. Make use of their knowledge and facilities. Accessing the internet is also a fantastic source of information about careers and job opportunities.

5. **Try volunteering** ... Many people find a route into full time work, or at the very least get valuable experience, by getting involved in voluntary organizations. Voluntary work also impresses potential employers.

# Topic 18: Effective methods of getting a job

## TOPIC IN ACTION

Read through the whole handout.

Now that the students have begun to look at the sorts of things that they would be attracted too as a career (or reinforced their ideas in the case of some), it's time to get some goal setting under way.

Here they could prepare an action plan around their future working life. They could also explore which of the EI and enterprise competencies will be useful to them (probably all of them!).

You could also encourage them to do some research about somebody they admire to see what steps they took.

## ACTIVITY 1

Divide the group into pairs.

Get them each to prepare a letter to a job agency, in which they express a desire for some holiday work. They need to list their strengths, qualities and experiences, and the sorts of work they would like to be considered for.

## Topic 19: Improving your job hunting success

'Success is not a result of spontaneous combustion. You must set yourself on fire.'

Reggie Leach

1. **There are jobs out there, including the ideal one for you** . . . Improve your chances by practising your hunting skills. Talk to successful job hunters who have been in your position. How did they do it? Get as much experience as you can, it's good for your learning and it will impress potential employers.

2. **Keep your options open** . . . Have other ways of describing yourself and your skills, alternative avenues, leads, targets and approaches.

3. **The more time you spend on your job hunt the more likely you are to get what you want** . . . Obvious perhaps, but it is suggested that you make your job hunt a full time occupation when the time comes.

4. **Target small companies and plenty of them** . . . See as many people as you can. Don't be dismayed by rejection. There are those that will not employ you for all sorts of reasons, but there are also those that will. When you meet the latter, it's up to you to tell them why they need you in their company and what you can offer them.

5. **Remember, don't get discouraged, accept it might take time and persist. Develop the skill of bouncing back from any setbacks.**

# Topic 19: Improving your job hunting success

## TOPIC IN ACTION

Read through the handout for further reinforcement. It is also designed to boost positive thinking.

Make the link between inner confidence, knowing who you are and what you want, and using the advice given in this session on how best to sell yourself.

It is very important to keep stressing that there is the right job out there for everybody, and that there are two kinds of employers ... those that won't give you a job for a variety of reasons (so forget about them) and those that will (Give all your focus to them!).

Use examples, if possible, to back up your advice.

Take any questions.

## Aim

This session moves on to how to deal effectively with interviews, both before and during. By preparing and rehearsing interviews, confidence and familiarity with the necessary skills grows. The students also benefit from trying their hand at being both an interviewee and interviewer during the role play part of the session.

## Materials

Three handouts: Before the interview; During the interview; The most common questions asked at interviews.
Flip chart and pens.
Room with space for group work.

## What happens?

Presentation by facilitator, discussion with students, role play, individual work.

## EI and enterprise competencies covered:

Self-awareness, self-responsibility, confidence, curiosity, initiative, dealing with uncertainty, positive and appreciative, courageous.

# Topic 20: Before the interview

'You have to know what you want to get.'

Gertrude Stein

1. **Research thoroughly** . . . Find out the following: What's the company's history and current situation? What are the specific details of the job on offer? Who will be interviewing you and what they are like? Why do you think this is the right job for you? Will it make you happy? Remember preparation really pays off.

2. **Prepare to project your key qualities and skills** . . . those that are just right for the job in question. Examine what they are looking for, and what you have to offer that will fit the bill. Don't hold back – be proud of what you have to offer, but don't fake it and pretend to be something you really know you are not.

3. **Anticipate possible questions** . . . Put yourself in the interviewer's shoes. Prepare questions that you would like to ask as well.

4. **Perfect your performance** . . . Practise. Look at your non-verbal communication skills as well as what you want to say. Use a mirror, video or voice recorder. Use friends. The better prepared you are the better you feel and the higher your self-esteem and confidence.

5. **Use creative visualization techniques** . . . Imagine yourself having a really successful interview, performing well and being offered and accepting the job. Imagine as vividly as you can how you would feel. Creative visualization does not of course guarantee success, but it gets you in a confident and positive frame of mind.

# Topic 20: Before the interview

## TOPIC IN ACTION

The previous session looked at the importance of research, in order to find jobs that match an individual's needs and strengths. It also described the impact of first impressions and the importance of image. The topics in this session reinforce and further develop this information.

Mention that creative visualization is dealt with later in the sessions, and that as a technique it can help create that all important positive attitude. In brief, this technique gets you to tap into your imagination to create a positive outcome to a forthcoming event. It can also be used as a tool for de-stressing.

To demonstrate how not to behave in an interview, set up a role play situation with another student or guest if you have one, where they interview you for a job. Do it really badly!

Get the students to note how many things you do wrong. For example, conflicting body language, poor first impression, ignorance of the company and job, obvious lack of preparation, inability to project key skills, chewing gum, taking mobile calls, scruffy appearance.

## ACTIVITY 1

Get each student to prepare for a short interview (approximately three minutes) where they are hoping to be taken onto the books of a job agency for holiday work.

They need to concentrate on selling themselves, making a strong first impression, explaining clearly what they are looking for and coming across generally as a confident positive and employable person.

Get them to list at least four adjectives that describe what sort of impression they wish to make. For example: enthusiastic, interested, knowledgeable, friendly, helpful, and prepare a key statement of what makes them highly employable. For example, 'I am reliable, trustworthy and enthusiastic. I take pride in the work I do and I believe I will be an asset to any company that offers me a position.'

Finally, get each one to make a list of the questions they would ask if they were the interviewer.

# Topic 21: During the interview

'It ain't what you say, it's the way that ya say it.'

Louis Armstrong

1. **Arrive with time to spare** ... so that you do not feel rushed, and remember that the 'interview' starts the minute you walk in the building. Turn your mobile off, sit down, relax, take deep breaths and mentally rehearse the impression you want to make. Use visualization or relaxation techniques to get you in the right frame of mind.

2. **Communicate with confidence** ... No matter how good your talents, knowledge, and ambitions, you need to get your message across effectively in the time you have.

3. **Dress to impress** ... Think carefully about the message you are sending out via your clothes, accessories and general appearance. It might seem wrong to place such importance on the 'wrapping', and to make value judgements, but that's the way it is. Don't fake it, just make the very best of yourself.

4. **Show you have done your homework** ... that you have researched the company, and most important you have the qualities they are looking for in an employee. Don't be afraid to ask questions, or consider your requirements, after all you also need to be sure this is the right job for you too. However, it is wise not to ask about money or holiday entitlement at this stage!

5. **Be aware of the power of non-verbal communication** ... Don't let your body language be at odds with what you are saying. Firm handshakes, good eye contact, a smile, upright posture, all these things count.

# Topic 21: During the interview

## TOPIC IN ACTION

It's time now to put the preparation into practice. You can begin by showing how to perform well in an interview.

Get feedback. Ask what was good about your performance.

## ACTIVITY 1

### 'Stop/cut'

Get two volunteers.

The scenario is a young person at an interview for summer work at a job agency.

The interviewer plays it straight but the interviewee must make as many mistakes as possible. For example, through scruffy appearance, chewing, yawning, taking mobile calls, sprawling posture, disinterested answers, etc.

Whenever the interviewee makes a mistake the students call out 'cut' or 'stop', say what is wrong and suggest how it should be done.

## ACTIVITY 2

### Emotional charades

This activity is about the power of non-verbal communication.

Enlist the help of about eight students, giving each a piece of paper on which is written emotional words, for example, nervous, confident, depressed, happy, etc.

They have to convey the word without speech, via their body language, while the rest of the group guesses the word.

To make it a little competitive you can divide them into teams to see who gets the most right in the shortest time.

A similar activity can be done, using words, tone and expression, to see how the meaning of a word like 'no' can be said in many different ways, or again use the phrase 'blah blah blah'.

## ACTIVITY 3

Divide the students into groups of three, so that in turn they are the interviewer, interviewee and observer.

It is the job of the observer to give constructive feedback on the performance of the interviewee.

# Topic 22: The most common questions asked at interviews

'In order to be irreplaceable, one must always be different.'

Coco Chanel

1. **Why are you here?** . . . In other words, why have you chosen our company to find a job?

2. **What can you do for us?** . . . Do you have skills and areas of knowledge that will be beneficial to us?

3. **What kind of person are you?** . . . Will you fit in? Do you get along with people? Will you be enjoyable to work with?

4. **Why should we offer you the job rather than somebody else?** . . . What makes you stand out from the others? What makes you special?

5. **Are you going to be good value for money?** . . . and will you be happy with what we are offering.

# Topic 22: The most common questions asked at interviews

## TOPIC IN ACTION

Take the students through the handout.

Emphasize that although interviews can be nerve-racking affairs, there is pressure too on those interviewing to make sure they make the right choice.

Also, don't forget that if you are the interviewee, you can also ask questions and decide whether or not you actually want the job if it is offered to you.

## Aim

The aim of this session is to encourage the students to understand the importance of managing stress, and to learn how to be motivated and adaptable. It also looks at the benefits of getting inspired by the stories of others.

## Materials

Three handouts: Motivation and adaptability; Stress busting; Getting inspired.
Flip chart and pens.
Room with space for group discussion.

## What happens?

Presentation by teacher/facilitator, discussion group and individual work.

## EI and enterprise competencies covered:

Self-awareness and self-responsibility, motivation, persistence, courage, positive and appreciative, confidence, dealing with uncertainty, curious, creative, using initiative.

# Topic 23: Motivation and adaptability

'Nothing endures but change.'

Heraclitus

'Be like a postage stamp, stick at one thing until you get there.'

Josh Billings

1. **Every day try to play to your strengths and work at your weaknesses** ... Invest in yourself. Have a plan, see what opportunities there are for you and grab them.

2. **See if you can always give a little more than is expected of you** ... Stretch yourself.

3. **Getting on is not just about doing things well, it's also about how you get on with others and having a good attitude** ... So get the recipe right – good knowledge and skills + good people skills and the right attitude = success.

4. **See everything you do as a step in your journey to the sort of life you want to have** ... Set goals to show how you would like your career and future to progress. If you are ambitious, say so and take action. If you are still not sure what you want, that's OK but keep yourself open to opportunities. It's all about deciding what you truly want for your life and taking the right action to get it.

5. **Things are always changing** ... Be self-aware, understand yourself, try to anticipate what will happen next, be open and proactive, and take responsibility for your future. Staying motivated and adaptable helps you on the road to success and makes you a valuable team member.

# Topic 23: Motivation and adaptability

## TOPIC IN ACTION

The aim is to encourage the students to take control of the situations they find themselves in, and be proactive.

It is very important that they are encouraged to take responsibility for the way they feel about themselves, their attitudes and the way they perform.

Generally people resist change, because they like to stay in their comfort zones. However, life and the world of work are constantly and swiftly changing, so adaptability is a very useful quality to possess.

The Motivation and adaptability handout offers sound advice on how to be successful and to continue to grow and develop.

## ACTIVITY 1

In pairs, get the students to quickly write down 5–10 qualities that they possess that would be valuable to an employer. If they get stuck, encourage them to ask for help from their fellow students or you so that further strengths can be uncovered.

Then get them each to read out those strengths to their partners – it helps to mentally reinforce ownership of them!
OR
If time allows get them to design a creative scene or poster to demonstrate the importance of either motivation, change or adaptability.

# Topic 24: Stress busting

'One way to get high blood pressure is to go mountain climbing over molehills.'

Earl Wilson

1. **Stress is part of life and is our natural reaction to what life throws at us** . . . *So* how you deal with stress is what counts and how you maintain a healthy balance is what matters. The most important thing is not to ignore stress when you are feeling it.

2. **Don't compare yourself or your situation with others** . . . because there is no right or wrong with stress levels. When your thoughts register fear or challenge or threat your body releases 'stressors' to help you cope and everybody responds to different things and to different degrees.

3. **Understand yourself** . . . Explore what releases your stressors and what your symptoms are. Make a list, and then take time to look at ways in which you can get support. Better still, how can you find ways to change your attitude so that you can help yourself to reduce the impact they have?

4. **Learn how to relax, get organized, reframe and take things one step at a time** . . . are four wonderful keys to releasing and reducing stress in our lives. Also try not to worry about things that you can't do anything about. Here you can use the area of influence and the area of concern (Activity 2) to help you.

5. **Be kind to yourself** . . . Make use of other techniques for dealing with stress. For example: share your worries with a sympathetic friend; distract yourself by doing something else; treat yourself to something you like; work on adopting a new attitude; get plenty of sleep. Don't beat yourself up! At any time when you feel unable to cope, ask yourself, is this really the end of the world? Be determined to take control of stressful thoughts. They are your thoughts so show them who is boss.

EMOTIONAL INTELLIGENCE AND ENTERPRISE HANDBOOK
© CHERYL BUGGY (CONTINUUM 2008)

# Topic 24: Stress busting

## TOPIC IN ACTION

Introduce the subject by explaining that stress is complicated. It is our body's instinctive reaction to change, threats, fears, problems and the general events and circumstances in our lives.

Begin by brainstorming with the students what things or situations in life could be called stressful. For example:

@ loss of a relationship

@ bullying

@ abuse

@ death

@ examinations

@ loss of a job

@ interview

@ changes in routine

@ moving house

@ holidays

@ promotion

@ falling in love/rejection

@ bad behaviour of others

@ the media/news

@ a sports match or competition

@ going on the stage

@ money worries

@ divorce

@ change and the unknown

Emphasize the point that some stress in life is both normal and necessary. Our stress reactions supply us with a certain type of energy, a natural stimulant called adrenaline, that enables us to deal with potentially threatening situations. The problem arises when our stress reactions happen too often and get out of control.

Stress can be our friend. If we stay in control in challenging situations, it can bring out the best in us. But if we let the situation distress us, it throws us into panic and overwhelms us. Remember there is no right or wrong with stress, it is how you deal with it that counts.

## ACTIVITY 1

Get the students to make a list of what commonly stresses people. Then get them to list symptoms of stress. The symptoms could be: eating too much or too little; lack of sleep; short temper; tears; low self-esteem; headaches; possibly other physical disorders.

Then get them to work with a partner, or on their own if they prefer, to develop strategies to help manage, or even eliminate the levels of the stress in the areas that cause them personal concern.

OR

Write up on the flip chart some of the common stress inducers given to you by the students, and get them to offer suggestions to reduce or eliminate them.

OR

Get them to design a stress prevention, or a stress busting poster or article for a student magazine.

OR

Get them to design letters and responses to and from an 'agony aunt' on teen stress related issues.

## ACTIVITY 2

## Area of concern and area of influence

This powerful technique, enables the user to get some perspective in times of worry and stress. It helps focus energy and attention on what can be done rather than worry and fret uselessly about things that the individual can have no impact on at that moment in time.

Draw, on the flip chart, a large circle with a smaller circle inside it. This is another version of the fried egg shape used in the comfort zone activity. Write at the top of the small circle Area of Influence and at the top of the large circle Area of Concern.

Use an example of your own to show the technique in operation, then get the students to try it for themselves. The idea is to take an issue that is causing worry or stress and decide whether anything can actually, practically be done about it.

If the answer is no, then put it in the area of concern section of the circle and mentally let go of it. If, on the other hand, there is something that can be done, then put it in the area of influence and then name the action you can take. An example might be that you are worried about global warming. You worrying about it is not having any positive effect on the planet whatsoever. So you can either take action by joining a group like Friends of the Earth, thereby moving it into your area of influence, or, whenever you catch yourself fretting about it, simply ask the worry to go away and stop yourself thinking about it. On a more personal topic, you could be worried about an interview you are about to have. Worrying will not help you be successful but preparing and working on your confidence and positive attitude will. So you can take action and therefore move the worry into your area of influence.

Finally emphasize how important it is to treat yourself with a little tender loving care. We are often far too hard on ourselves, and by failing to care for ourselves, or tackle problems, or have a healthy lifestyle and outlook, allow stress to get out of control.

## Topic 25: Getting inspired

'You see things and say "Why?". But I dream things that never were and I say "Why not?".'

George Bernard Shaw

1. **Other people's stories can be invaluable in helping spur you on towards your own success** . . . Their actions and beliefs can show you the ropes, show you what might work and what might not and generally give you advice and encouragement through their own experiences.

2. **The ideal 'inspirer' might be one that is in the same field or occupation you are interested in** . . . You could research their stories through the internet or library.

3. **However, don't be exclusive** . . . Be curious about people in other walks of life too, not just those you are interested in. It's often not so much what people do, but how they feel and what they believe that you can learn from.

4. **So be prepared to learn and be inspired from the experiences and advice of those you admire** . . . if it feels right. Learn from their successes and failures. You can also ask for their advice and support to help you grow. You will be amazed how many people will be happy to give you advice if you only have the courage to ask.

5. **Inspire others** . . . You would be amazed how your story can positively influence others. That in turn can make you feel great!

EMOTIONAL INTELLIGENCE AND ENTERPRISE HANDBOOK
© CHERYL BUGGY (CONTINUUM 2008)

# Topic 25: Getting inspired

## TOPIC IN ACTION

## ACTIVITY 1

Get the students to work in pairs. The task is to draw up a list of qualities that would make their partner inspiring for a Year 7 pupil. For example, friendly, knowledgeable, funny, helpful, good listener.

These lists can be exhibited on the walls as a good confidence booster at the end of the session.

OR

Design a poster or flyer called Secrets of Success, that shows the key qualities of somebody that inspires them. Use the twelve competencies as a guideline.

OR

Imagine they are writing a letter about themselves set 15 years in the future. What would their story be in terms of what they have achieved and what advice they would give to a student of their age now.

OR

If they were setting up their own business what would it be? There is a saying, 'From little acorns, big oak trees grow'. Do they have a small simple idea that could lead to a successful business? An example to cite would be the windsurfing students who adapted a watch strap using Velcro and from that the Animal brand was born. Or similarly the students who took a bag of home made tee shirts on a skiing trip to pay for their holiday and the Fat Face Company was born.

## Aim

In this, the final session of the course, the focus is on drawing together the threads by tackling the inner blockages and mindsets that can so hamper the journey to fulfilment and success. The first subject tackled is problems, and the object is to develop an understanding and perspective on the subject, as well as offering tips on how to deal with problems when they inevitably come along. Further advice then helps the students look towards achieving their hopes, goals and dreams by using creative visualization techniques. The session concludes by showing ways to develop winning attitudes, because after all, the aim of this programme is to produce winners who will make the very most of their potential.

## Materials

Four handouts: Dealing with problems; Achieving your hopes, dreams and goals; Creative visualization and How to be a winner.
Flip chart and pens.
Room with space for group work.

## What happens?

Presentation by teacher/facilitator, group discussion, individual and group work.

## EI and enterprise competencies covered:

All of them!

# Topic 26: Dealing with problems

'The quitter never wins and the winner never quits.'

Napolean Hill

1. **Life will always throw problems at you, they are totally normal** ... They can often be solved and are not always bad news! It's how you look at a problem that counts, and the key to that is ...

2. **Believe in yourself** ... Don't say 'It's too difficult, I'm not up to it'. Be confident; you have all you need inside yourself to overcome most problems. Use your brain, your experience and your intelligence to help you. Don't let fear and confusion push you around!

3. **Keep trying different approaches to your problem** ... Every problem has a soft spot where you can 'attack' it, so persist and find it. Don't panic, keep calm. Then deal with it a step at a time.

4. **Accentuate the positive, eliminate the negative** ... If you think in a negative way you will often attract negative results. Keep telling yourself that you can deal with and solve any problem that comes along in a positive way.

5. **It's often too soon to quit** ... Don't be threatened or overwhelmed by your problem. Persist, and say 'I can handle this!' That might mean asking for help, and don't ever be afraid to do that. Finally, remember that you can learn from every single problem that you experience in your life.

EMOTIONAL INTELLIGENCE AND ENTERPRISE HANDBOOK
© CHERYL BUGGY (CONTINUUM 2008)

# Topic 26: Dealing with problems

## TOPIC IN ACTION

The word 'problem' is a very interesting one, by virtue of the fact that some perceive it as a fearful and threatening word, while others see it as something that represents challenge and excitement.

Throughout this programme we have seen how our mindset, the way we have been programmed to think and react, can limit our potential. However, we have also learned that any behaviour is learned behaviour, and what has been learned can be unlearned.

Use your stories to reinforce this message, by drawing on personal experiences or the stories of others.

Address the first point on the handout, making it clear that problems will always exist in life, but it is down us how we choose to perceive and deal with any 'problem'. Try to get the students to give you examples from their own personal experiences of a time when a problem turned out not to be a problem at all once it was challenged, or a time when they overcame a problem and learned from it. Explore how problems in the past have made them feel, and how they could have had a different outlook from the wisdom of hindsight.

In point two, show how the EI and enterprise competencies help enormously when dealing with problems.

In point three, brainstorm a problem with the group. The point of the activity is to allow a free flowing of ideas so that the 'soft spot' of the problem can be found, and a variety of solutions offered. For example, a student can't decide what course to take when they leave school, or is overwhelmed by work pressure or has fallen out with a parent.

Refer back to the session on fears, because fears, like problems, do not simply go away if you ignore them.

One of the keys is to change the way you perceive a problem. If you take charge and see it as a challenge, you can then search, like a detective, for an answer.

The final point is based on the fact that people often give up when they are so close to solving their problem, so it is often too soon to quit!

# Topic 27: Achieving your hopes, dreams and goals

'In life, as in football, you won't go far unless you know where the goalposts are.'

Arnold Glasow

1. **First you need to have a sharply focused goal or dream** . . . So what is it? If you were told that you could not fail, what would you go for? And the answer is not winning the lottery!

2. **To be successful you have to have a deep desire** . . . and you have got to really, really want it, every bit of you has got to want it. That deep desire is your driving force.

3. **Practise creative visualization** . . . Picture your goal or dream, and fix it in your mind. You can become that which you constantly imagine yourself to be or have, so see yourself there, or having what you want and feel yourself there.

4. **Work on your beliefs** . . . If you expect the worst and are fearful, you stop trying, and grind to a halt. In the law of attraction, what you send out, you draw back to yourself to confirm your beliefs. You cannot really afford too many negative thoughts if you want to achieve your goal or dream.

5. **Meet setbacks** . . . by understanding what happened, formulating a clear plan, believing in yourself, keeping sharply focused, picturing your goal clearly in your mind, and refusing to be defeated.

# Topic 27: Achieving your hopes, dreams and goals

## TOPIC IN ACTION

If you talk to successful people, you discover that they have not become successful by accident. Generally they have had a goal, or series of goals, which they have backed up with passion, hard work and determination. Also, although money might be important to them, it is not generally central to their life. It's almost as if they have followed their interests and passions and the money has followed. These people also tend to have strong self-belief, feel good about themselves, see problems as challenges and are able to bounce back from setbacks.

## ACTIVITY 1

Set the students the individual task of writing about their perfect day, based on the assumption that a magic wand has been waved and they can create whatever they want.

In pairs, get the students to share what they have written. Putting something into writing and speaking it out loud helps to reinforce it.

The next step is to make a list of what has to be done in order to manifest the perfect day in terms of attitudes and actions. Get the students to help each other with this if necessary.

See if any students want to share their perfect day and their action plan. You could put up all the 'perfect days' around the room as a positive 'feel good' statement.

Students could be given new exercise books that can become their record of their journey towards their perfect day, or as a celebration of all of the good things that have happened/are happening in their lives. For example, they could write a list of their blessings, such as family, friends, health, home, education. Also they could add their list of values and a mission statement. A mission statement provides a powerful focus and anchor for what somebody wants for their life. Here are a couple of examples: 'I will love myself and my family, care about my life and about the world, stand up for my beliefs and fight for my dreams'. Or, 'I am special and I will make a difference to the world'.

## ACTIVITY 2

Divide the students into groups of four or five and get them to devise guidelines for achieving goals, hopes and dreams around the mnemonic SUCCESS.

For example:

S – search for a dream.
U – understand what makes you feel good.
C – concentrate on what you want.
C – cope with setbacks along the way.
etc.

Put the results around the walls.

## Topic 28: Creative visualization

'Imagination is more important than knowledge. It's a preview of life's coming attractions.'

Albert Einstein

1. **Creative visualization can help you change your most basic attitudes to life** . . . You have all you need to begin the process in your mind. All you have to do is tap into your imagination and get it working for you.

2. **You tap into your imagination by asking it to develop pictures and stories for you** . . . It's always more than happy to oblige. Begin by relaxing, try counting from one to ten, sit in a comfortable position, close your eyes and play some appropriate music. When you feel ready and your body is relaxed, imagine something you would really like. Use all your senses to get in touch with it. Make the experience as real and as vivid as you can.

3. **Whatever you focus your attention on, can grow** . . . and it's the reason creative visualization works. We always seem to attract into our lives whatever we think about most, believe in most strongly and expect or imagine most vividly. Your unconscious mind cannot distinguish between fact and fantasy. Think how often your dreams have seemed very real!

4. **In order to visualize successfully you need to do four basic things** . . . Set your goal, create a very clear idea or picture, focus on it as often as you can and feed it with plenty of positive statements and thoughts.

5. **Help creative visualization along by taking action** . . . It's a great exercise, but by itself it isn't enough. You also need to do whatever you can to practically help you achieve your goals.

# Topic 28: Creative visualization

## TOPIC IN ACTION

If you ask most successful athletes, or people in the business world, you will find that this is a technique that they regularly use. If it is something you use, explain how and why.

Take the students through points one to five, inviting any questions.

Visualization is a wonderfully powerful process that anybody can use, at any time. It can be implemented for a variety of reasons. It requires the user to tap into the power of their imagination, to 'visualize', for example, a positive outcome to an event like an interview, or a state of being in order to feel better, for example, calm. The imagination is so powerful it can create a physiological change in the body without any real action taking place.

## ACTIVITY 1

### Perfect place – a visualization for relaxation

Play some peaceful music, dim the lights.

Relax the body.

Take deep regular breaths.

Imagine a perfect location where you would feel wonderful, like a beach, mountain top or woodland.

Imagine what you can see – focus on shapes and colours. Imagine what you can hear and smell. Imagine what you might feel on your skin – sunlight, breeze, etc.

Now focus on how you are feeling – relaxed, calm, happy, peaceful, elated, safe, etc. Enjoy the feeling and try to magnify it so it spreads throughout the whole body.

After five minutes, come mentally back into the room, stretch and take a deep breath.

Some students might find this difficult or be resistant, so make the point that if visualization is good enough for Olympic gold medalists, it might be worth giving it a try!

Encourage the students to experiment with this technique at home. It's not so very far from daydreaming, except with this technique, you control your thoughts and can always have a positive outcome.

## Topic 29: How to be a winner

'Losers visualise the penalties of failure. Winners visualise the rewards of success.'

Dr Rob Gilbert

1. **Winners take responsibility for their lives** ... They are not moaners, and do not constantly blame others and events for what happens to them. They never start with a negative or make endless excuses.

2. **Winners make things happen** ... They invent their own futures. They set goals, they anticipate success, they work hard and they practise hard. They live in the present moment rather than dwell in the past or worry about the future.

3. **Winners know that you have to feel good in order to do well** ... They like and understand themselves, know how to play to their strengths, and are not afraid to pat themselves on the back when they perform well.

4. **Winners dwell on the rewards of success not the penalty of failure** ... For them optimism is their natural state, they produce their own 'highs'. They realize that how they feel has a huge impact on what they do and how they respond to the world around them.

5. **Winners know it's how you take what happens to you in life that is what counts** ... They are able to cope with whatever comes their way because they know that even a crisis can be seen as an opportunity, and a mistake is a chance to learn a useful lesson.

# Topic 29: How to be a winner

## TOPIC IN ACTION

Throughout this programme you have been encouraging the students to take responsibility for their lives as much as possible. The world is full of victims, we don't need any more.

We tend to live in a 'blame' culture, with a media that focuses on bad news, where it is always somebody else's fault. We also live in a climate where some people abdicate responsibility for their lives, the choices they make and the actions they take. Surely what we all want is young people who can think for themselves and make positive choices for now and in the future.

In a way the five points on this final handout sum it up!

## TECHNIQUE

### Affirmations

Affirmations are words or phrases repeated over and over to get into a different, positive and determined mental state. It is a technique much used in sport psychology.

Affirmations need to be:

@ positive

@ present tense

@ personal

@ used often

Examples:

@ I can do this!

@ I am a strong and powerful person!

@ I am going to have a good day!

@ Whatever happens I can handle it!

@ I like myself.

## Reframing

This technique helps the user to see a situation in a different and more positive light. It is literally a case of exploring an issue from a different angle or perspective. The following phrases can be used as examples:

@ 'They won't allow that' can become 'I can try to persuade them'.

@ 'If only' can become 'When' or 'I will make this happen'

@ 'I can't' can become 'I will' or 'I will try'.

@ 'I must' can become 'I will' or 'I want to'.

@ 'I have to get up' can become 'Good, a new day!' or 'I'm going to get up and have a great day'.

## ACTIVITY 1

Encourage the students to create an action plan of how they are going to make changes using the five headings from the handout as their guidelines.

Aim for three changes per point. For example, 'I am going to take responsibility for my life by changing some of the negative thinking habits I have. Thoughts such as "I am useless at getting organized and I will never lose weight" will become "I will make things happen by setting time aside every week to tidy my room, and set myself the goal of losing half a stone in a month".

They might add beside each point the competencies they could use to help them, and any of the tools and techniques they have learned about during the programme that would be of assistance. For example: being positive and appreciative, using initiative, applying affirmations, using the areas of influence and concern, reframing, etc.

## ACTIVITY 2

## Food for thought

Here are two examples of advice from successful people. After reading it, the student could be encouraged to find somebody to interview to add to the advice below.

## How to be successful in business by David Henley

@ Do something that you really love and feel passionate about.

@ Develop sound interpersonal skills, particularly in the areas of leadership and relationship building.

@ Wherever possible choose influencers, i.e. people whom you respect and admire and take note of how they go about their business.

@ In making decisions try to recognize the 'big picture' and how even small decisions lead towards much larger objectives.

@ Don't be afraid to try many ideas. Make a conscious effort to develop those which you believe would be successful, although you must expect some of them to die.

@ Try to recognize in any organization where you fit in and whether you enjoy the culture.

## Keys to maximizing your working potential by Gael Lindenfield

@ Maintain a high degree of self-esteem – taking great care to look after your own health and welfare and keep 'in tune' with your own values.

@ Think and talk positively about yourself and others, as well as work.

@ Set challenging but realistic goals – both for the short term and long term.

@ Become highly organized and take care to be tidy.

@ Structure your time with care, leaving aside some 'free-floating' space for creativity and relaxation.

@ Constantly improve and update your communication and self-presentation skills.

@ Be assertive as often as you can but retain the right to use passivity when necessary.

@ Carefully monitor and control your stress levels.

@ Regularly review and nurture your working relationships.

@ Set aside regular times for self-appraisal and constructive critical feedback from others.

@ Be constantly committed to ongoing personal and professional development and training.

You could also encourage the students to come up with their own list of advice and call it Tips for Those Who Want to be Winners.

## CONCLUDING THE PROGRAMME

Take some time to recap on the key points of the programme, and complete any unfinished business.

A suggestion might be for them to describe their perfect day and then explain what initial steps they are going to take to move towards achieving that perfect day. They could also proudly share the qualities they now know they possess from the EI and enterprise competencies list.

To conclude, sit the group in a circle, asking each in turn to share what for them has been the most valuable part of the programme, and what they feel the future now holds for them.

# Supplementary activities

## ICE BREAKERS AND TEAM ACTIVITIES

### Ice breakers

You can use 'ice breakers' at any time, for example in Session 1 to 'kick start' the process, or when you want to re-energize the group. You may have your own favourite ice breakers, but here are some examples:

- Who are you? – Hand out bags of belongings, one for each table of students. Ask them about the individual who owns the belongings based on the questions you will find in Topic 16, Activity 1.

- Get the students in a circle, with a soft ball available. A student begins by saying a positive thing about themselves and then throws the ball to somebody else to do the same. A variation on this is for the ball to be thrown to somebody and the thrower pays a compliment to the person they are throwing to. Or you could sit a student in the middle of a circle and everybody has to pay them a compliment.

- In groups of about six to eight, give each student a piece of paper. On it they write the name of the person to their left and add a compliment. They then fold and pass to the left. The group keeps going until each student receives their named paper along with a list of compliments. A variation on this is for you to give the students the first line in a story, and they each have to add a sentence, fold and pass. It's creative and fun!

- Get one student to stand at one corner of the room with another student at the other end of the room so that they are diagonally opposite. Take a theme and get one student to argue for and one against. After a little while get the rest of the students to stand somewhere on the imaginary line between the two depending on how they feel about the issue. An example might be 'You should never tell on your mates, even if you know one of them has done something that has harmed somebody else.' Or 'Everybody should have to vote once they reach voting age.' This activity gets students to consider their values.

## Team activities

### Tower building activity (see Topic 15)

Get the students into teams.

Give them either: playing cards; straws and marshmallows: spaghetti and marshmallows; or old newspapers or straws and Sellotape.

Give them 15 minutes or so to build the tallest freestanding tower using the items they have. Or you can add a hard boiled egg to see which group can use straws and Sellotape to make the egg roll the furthest.

### Red/black game (see Topic 15)

This game is a great practical example of how teams do or do not work. It only really works well if both groups realize that this is not a competition but a collaborative activity. Usually, however, it becomes a hotly contested 'fight' where focus on the task becomes lost in mistrust and a siege mentality. Remember you can only play this game once!

TASK: To end up with a positive score for your group.

PROCEDURE: The Trainer will visit your group and ask you to decide whether to play RED or to play BLACK. The Trainer will not tell you which colour the other group has played.

When both groups have declared their play, the Trainer will announce the colours which have been played.

Play will be scored as follows:

| IF GROUP 1 PLAYS | AND GROUP 2 PLAY | THE SCORE IS | |
|---|---|---|---|
| | | GROUP 1 | GROUP 2 |
| RED | RED | +3 | +3 |
| RED | BLACK | −6 | +6 |
| BLACK | RED | +6 | −6 |
| BLACK | BLACK | −6 | −6 |

There will be ten rounds. After the fourth round the Trainer will ask the groups whether they wish to have a conference. This conference will only take place at the request of both groups. If either does not wish to confer then no meeting will take place.

After the eighth round there will be a second opportunity for a conference, should both groups wish it.

The ninth and tenth rounds score double.

### Air crash activity (see Topic 15)

This is a challenging activity that not only requires members of the team to work together to achieve the objective, it requires participants to make decisions, to persuade others of the reasons for their decisions and to negotiate with others to achieve a consensus.

Your light aeroplane is forced down on a flight over the Baird Mountains between the Baring Strait and Anchorage in Alaska.

You have been on a business trip, and so you are not appropriately dressed for the January weather, with temperatures typically −7°C, around the coldest in the world for the time of year.

A small group of you have survived the crash and have managed to evacuate the aeroplane, which is now burnt out. However, you have been able to rescue a number of items from the plane, which, in the necessary haste, you felt might be useful.

You know the pilot was unable to call for help on the radio before the crash, and also that, from the windows, there appeared to be no signs of habitation for as far as the eye could see.

Your task is to decide, first as an individual, and then as a group, the priority of each of the rescued items in the struggle for your continued survival and rescue (20 minutes total time allowed).

NB. There is no other equipment available to you other than what you would normally carry about your person, and none of you has any particular experience in survival methods.

## Equipment list

| ITEM | YOU | TEAM | EXPERT | YOU | TEAM |
|------|-----|------|--------|-----|------|
| JACK KNIFE | | | | | |
| SECTIONAL AIR MAP | | | | | |
| RIFLE & AMMUNITION | | | | | |
| PLASTIC SHEET 9' x 12' | | | | | |
| 4 PAIRS OF SUNGLASSES | | | | | |
| SMALL BOTTLE OF BRANDY | | | | | |
| COSMETIC MIRROR | | | | | |
| 12 PACKETS OF PEANUTS | | | | | |
| 1 PAIR OF SKIS | | | | | |
| 4 WOOL BLANKETS | | | | | |
| 1 METAL COFFEE POT | | | | | |
| FIRST AID KIT | | | | | |
| 3 BOOKS OF MATCHES | | | | | |
| FLASHLIGHT & BATTERIES | | | | | |
| 1 LARGE CANDLE | | | | | |

## Survival experts scoring

**photocopiable**

| ITEM | YOU | TEAM | EXPERT | YOU | TEAM |
|---|---|---|---|---|---|
| JACK KNIFE | | | 5 | | |
| SECTIONAL AIR MAP | | | 12 | | |
| RIFLE & AMMUNITION | | | 14 | | |
| PLASTIC SHEET 9' x 12' | | | 2 | | |
| 4 PAIRS OF SUNGLASSES | | | 10 | | |
| SMALL BOTTLE OF BRANDY | | | 15 | | |
| COSMETIC MIRROR | | | 7 | | |
| 12 PACKETS OF PEANUTS | | | 11 | | |
| 1 PAIR OF SKIS | | | 13 | | |
| 4 WOOL BLANKETS | | | 1 | | |
| 1 METAL COFFEE POT | | | 6 | | |
| FIRST AID KIT | | | 9 | | |
| 3 BOOKS OF MATCHES | | | 3 | | |
| FLASHLIGHT & BATTERIES | | | 8 | | |
| 1 LARGE CANDLE | | | 4 | | |

# Emotional intelligence competencies

 **SELF-AWARENESS**

- To become more self-aware you need to be a bit of a detective with yourself. It's a very worthwhile activity.

- Know what motivates you and avoid what demotivates you.

- Know what makes you happy and what gets you down, what stresses you, what excites you, what makes you feel calm and peaceful, angry or sad?

- Explore any attitudes or beliefs that you may have that could hold you back from what you want in life.

- What are your fears? What will happen if you let them dominate your life? How can you overcome them?

- What have you learned from your life experiences so far?

- If somebody was to come up to you and ask the following questions you will be able to answer them because you have done some 'homework' on yourself – What are your strengths? What would you like to be better at? What is your aim in life at this moment in time? How are you feeling right now and why?

 **SELF-RESPONSIBILITY**

- Listen to yourself, observe your chattering thoughts. Whenever you catch yourself using self-defeating language (something along the lines of I can't, I'm not good enough, it's too difficult, it's not fair, it's not my fault, he/she made me). Stop and give yourself some straight talking and try to ban such words from your inner conversation. Can you think of any inspiring person you know of who would go towards a situation using such language and expecting a positive outcome? Unlikely. Always try to replace negatives with words that are more, if not totally, positive. Positive self-talk is worth its weight in gold!

- Before you open your mouth try to really consider the words you are about to use. Try to never speak in anger, put people down, put yourself down, gossip, hurt or use any language that could damage the confidence and self-esteem of yourself or others.

- That does not mean you cannot be assertive and stand up for yourself or others,

EMOTIONAL INTELLIGENCE AND ENTERPRISE HANDBOOK
© CHERYL BUGGY (CONTINUUM 2008)

if you find something unacceptable. Always make sure you challenge in a respectful way.

- Research shows that for every one positive comment made to children as they are growing up they receive about fifty negative or less positive ones. That's why many people tend to have a more negative outlook on life than a positive one. So what can you do about words from the past? Well the past is the past and there is absolutely nothing you can do to change it. What you can do though is to deal with the things from the past to ensure they do not have a negative effect on your life now or in the future.

- To help you do that, if you can see that you are feeling upset, or negative as a result of something from the past, allow yourself to feel the feeling but only for a short time. In other words, feel the feeling and then ask it to go. Keep doing this until it begins to occur less and less. Finally it will disappear. Try then to forgive anybody who has said negative things, or done wrong to you in the past. Why? Because holding on to such things is damaging to you and holds you back. It can poison the present and damage your dreams. If things from the past have left your self-esteem damaged, or if you have simmering resentment, then you are allowing others to potentially ruin your life! NB. If you have been harmed or abused in the past, please get some safe, professional help. This will enable you to heal and move on.

- If somebody is being judgemental or having a bad day, if they are feeling angry, hurt, resentful or jealous, for example, they are likely to behave badly to others. They want to pay how they are feeling forward, and make others feel bad too, and they are often not even aware they are doing it. Don't be one of those people!

- If you are on the receiving end of such behaviour, here is what you can do. Listen carefully. If there is some truth in what is being said then take it on board and take positive action. For example, if you have done something that has upset somebody else and what you did was unfair then say sorry. If that is not the case then don't react. Practise empathy and understand that the other person might be coming from a difficult place at the moment and rise above it. Don't react, don't give them the satisfaction! As a result of controlling your responses you feel more confident and proud of yourself.

- Strive to nurture the positive feelings you have like joy, fun, happiness, contentment, peace, excitement, satisfaction. Whenever you feel such a feeling (and it's great if you can make your mind regularly create them) stay focused on them and notice how the feeling gets bigger and lasts longer.

- When you experience feelings that are not such good news, such as anger, fear, resentment, jealousy or anxiety, you need to take action to remove them from your system, or change them into something else because they are not good for you. To do that here is what you do: acknowledge what you are feeling, allow yourself to feel it for a little while or do something that will soothe you or in some way help you to move on. For example, if you are angry take some exercise, or write it down and out of your system. If you feel fearful, find somebody you trust who can help you talk yourself through the fear and out the other side. If you feel sad, have a good old cry and then focus on something that makes you feel that it's good to be alive.

- Some emotions are very, very powerful and overwhelming when you are experiencing them. Such things as a broken heart, grief at the death of a loved one or fear as a result of the way somebody has treated you are not going to pass overnight. In such cases it really is best if you can talk to someone who is trustworthy, skilled at giving good support and advice and who can protect you.

 ## POSITIVE AND APPRECIATIVE

- Maybe you have had some tough experiences in life that have made it difficult for you to be positive about things. Acknowledge that it is difficult for you, allow yourself to feel sad, let down, angry, in order to get it out of your system then move on! Don't spend the rest of your life trapped by your past.

- Focus on what you have, not what you have not got. In other words count your blessings, see all the good things in your life, like your family and friends, your home, your health, just being alive!

- Look back and see all that you have achieved so far and appreciate yourself. You have already accomplished so many things in your life, from learning to walk and talk, to more complex things like understanding how to use a computer or being good at a sport.

- Try to spend your time with positive people.

- Have some goals and dreams for your life.

- Keep learning and trying new things; it builds your confidence and therefore your optimism.

- Read about people who inspire you.

- Don't compare yourself unfavourably with others. Realize that everybody is unique, including you.

- Look after yourself and don't feed yourself junk food or junk experiences and thoughts. Remember junk in, junk out!

- Sell yourself the benefits of having a positive mental attitude (PMA). In other words, what is in it for you if you become more positive (WIIFM?)?

EMOTIONAL INTELLIGENCE AND ENTERPRISE HANDBOOK
© CHERYL BUGGY (CONTINUUM 2008)

- Always try to see the good in others.

# EMPATHETIC AND RESPECTFUL

- Try to become less upset or reactive to what others say by being less judgemental. Be more understanding and as a result people will not stress you out so much, and you will be happier.

- Make an effort to be more open minded. Challenge your beliefs and views – are you sure you are right? Could there be more ways of seeing a situation?

- Be interested in people, in everybody you meet or read about. It will mean you will learn more and have a greater awareness of others. This will also make you wiser and more knowledgeable.

- As your empathy grows so your relationships and friendships improve and you are likely to be more popular.

- Try putting yourself in somebody's shoes just for a moment before you speak to them. If you can try to work out what they may be thinking and feeling, you will become more empathetic and therefore a far more effective and influential communicator. You will also be very employable.

- Remember everybody has a right to their opinion, whether you agree with them or not.

- Think of the consequences of your actions on others. Are you being kind and thoughtful or careless, unkind and disruptive?

# MOTIVATED

- Spend some time deciding what your dream or vision for your life is. It can be an inspiring incentive to keep you going, especially when the going gets tough and you feel your motivation slipping. Capture it in a journal or collage to give you a constant visual reminder of what you want for yourself.

- If you are hanging back over something, take a moment to sell yourself the benefits. For example, 'If I get this piece of work done it will help me get the qualification I need, and I will have bought myself some free time to spend with my friends'.

- Find ways to help yourself when you experience setbacks or just feel demotivated. For example, it could be talking to a friend, taking time out and doing something completely different, buying yourself a treat or getting inspired by somebody else's story.

- Take things a step at a time. If you expect to make one single jump and be successful overnight then let me tell you now it's not going to happen. If you plan a series of actions and steps you can take to achieve your hopes and dreams they will keep you motivated.

- Celebrate every step towards your success and pat yourself on the back.

- Ask yourself, what sorts of things do I love doing, what sorts of things do I really not want to do?

- Have a plan which maps the steps that will get you moving closer to your dreams.

- Ask yourself, if I start taking those steps today what's the first one I will take? Then take it!

- Find out who can help you achieve what you want to achieve.

 **PERSISTENT**

- When attempting something, break it down into small manageable chunks so that it appears more achievable.

- Find out if somebody has already done it in the past and learn from what they did or didn't do.

- Get some personal cheerleaders, such as friends, family and staff at school/college, etc.

- Sell yourself the benefits of persisting. For example, just think how good you will feel when you move closer to achieving your goal and finally achieve it.

- Face any fear you might have around the issue. If you don't confront it it will not only not go away, it will get bigger and could even stop you in your tracks.

- Give yourself some treats to keep you going.

- Give yourself some breaks too, and space to re-energize.

- The more passionate or enthusiastic you are about something the more likely you are to persist at it.

- If you meet setbacks, don't be defeated. Understand what has happened, learn from it, then bounce back and keep trying.

EMOTIONAL INTELLIGENCE AND ENTERPRISE HANDBOOK
© CHERYL BUGGY (CONTINUUM 2008)

# Enterprise competencies

 ## USING INITIATIVE

- Remind yourself of all the things in your life you have already achieved because you have just got on with it.

- Get motivated. Find out what gets you excited, what gives you 'get up and go' energy.

- Read about inspirational people that you admire and learn from the actions they took to take control of their lives.

- Don't give in to any negative gremlin in your head that might be whispering that you could fail or might make a fool of yourself if you take action. Anyway, what if you do fail? It's quite rightly said, that the only failure is not trying in the first place!

- Don't spend time with people who get you down or who are stuck and too apathetic or frightened to just get on with their own lives. If you are not careful you can end up being a victim like them.

- It's difficult to use your initiative if you are tired and have not been looking after yourself.

- Help others by encouraging them to get on with their lives. By being positive and motivating for others you can feel energized and inspired to take action.

- Have a dream for your life and a plan of how you are going to achieve it.

- Keep challenging and stretching yourself in every area of your life. The more you grow, the more you face your fears, the more you expand and the more confident you feel and the more you will have the courage to use your initiative.

- Network, seize opportunities and if the opportunities don't arise, create them for yourself.

- Know what your strengths are – make a list. What are you good at? If you know yourself you are in a better position to act without having to consult others.

- Keep assertive, face your fears and learn to handle uncertainty and change.

- You have an amazing brain with billions of brain cells. So keep using it.

- Don't get stale or complacent or bland, keep using the why word. Be curious about yourself and why you are thinking and feeling the way you are. Ask yourself, what do I want from life and how am I going to get it? Ask how can I help others? Ask people about themselves; it might irritate them sometimes but you can live with that and you will learn a lot in the process!

- Develop eagle vision. Pull back from time to time and see the big picture of your life and where you want it to go.

- Try not to worry about the opinions of others or being judged or rejected.

 # DEALING WITH UNCERTAINTY

- Maintain a positive attitude and believe in yourself.

- Keep affirming to yourself that you are unique and special with plenty to offer the world whatever happens.

- Have the courage to take risks. Yes, you might feel scared, yes, you might worry you will fail or look stupid, but that's the way most people feel when they try something new. But just think how brilliant you will feel if you succeed at something new, and how much more confident you will become.

- Develop the ability to bounce back from setbacks and be resilient and persistent.

- Take time to think 'out of the box' and help yourself to do that by asking If?, Why not?, What if? and How? questions.

- Find out ways to keep yourself motivated; it will give you drive and energy and help you face the unknown.

- Keep flexible, responsive and open minded. Anticipate what might happen next and how you might benefit from it.

- There is a saying that goes 'There are three types of people in the world: those who make things happen, those who watch things happen and those who wonder what happened'. Try to be one of the first type if you want to deal positively with uncertainty.

- Use positive affirmations to help you face uncertainty, like 'Whatever happens I can handle it'.

 # CREATIVE

- Be resourceful – look at what you have at your disposal (qualities and experience and things) to help you to be creative in any situation.

- Use any method you can e.g. internet, the library, magazines, TV shows, talking to others, to get inspired and to explore how others have had creative ideas and turned them into creative actions.

- Sometimes doing absolutely nothing, or daydreaming when doing simple things like taking a shower or a stroll, can be one of the most creative things you do.

Your quiet or idling mind suddenly has the space to come up with great new ideas.

- Creatively network with others. Make a list of all the people you know so far in a special contacts book. Write down who they are and what they do and their contact details. This initial list might only contain the names and details of people in your family, your family's friends, your personal friends, and school and college staff, for example, but that's perfectly fine as a starter. You can add to that list by speaking to your initial contacts because all those people know other people, and so it goes on.

- The point of developing a network of contacts is that you can find how other people can help you, and explore what you have to offer and how you can help them.

- Design your two business cards. The first sums you up at this moment in time, and the second represents who you intend to become professionally.

- When being creative it helps to use the Who?, What?, When?, Why?, How?, What if? questions that inventors and entrepreneurs use all the time.

- Your brain struggles to be creative if you are over stressed, over tired, over emotional or if you are surrounded by mess and clutter.

- Sometimes being creative can start with one small silly step that might not even make any sense. Try it sometime, it could lead to something unusual.

- Don't be afraid to make mistakes or ask others for feedback and advice.

- Try changing your daily routine and do a few things at different times and in different ways.

 ## COURAGEOUS

- Remember all the times in the past when you have shown courage and been brave when trying something new or facing up to something.

- Name any fear you might have then ask yourself this: 'If I confront this fear what is the worst thing that can happen to me?' Is it likely to be the end of the world?

- Look at the advantages to you if you challenge and overcome a fear. How will you benefit?

- Look at ways in which you can help yourself challenge and overcome the fear. Who or what can help you? Make a list.

- Break the fear busting strategy into small bite-sized bits. Then tackle it one step at a time.

- Work on your confidence. Dealing with fear is much easier if you believe in yourself.

- Don't give yourself a hard time if you become overwhelmed by a fear but do be determined to deal with it, and not let it control you.

- Read stories to inspire you about people who have overcome their fears and achieved their goals. Remember anybody who has ever achieved anything will have had to deal with all sorts of fears in all sorts of shapes and sizes.

- Use positive self-talk (affirmations) to help you keep strong in the face of your fear. For example, say 'I will face my fear and do it anyway'. Or 'I am bigger than my fear'.

- Fears are natural and normal. Some fears are very helpful in keeping you safe but many only serve to keep you playing small. Be sure you know the difference in your own mind between the two.

- As long as you are developing and facing new situations fear will always be present. That's normal. It's the relationship you have with that fear that counts. Don't let it become some great monster that is standing in front of you and blocking your way. Courageously confront it!

- Every time you take a courageous step, celebrate.

 **CONFIDENT**

- Know what your values are and be clear how you want to be treated, how you will treat others, and what you want and will and will not tolerate.

- Respect yourself.

- Remember you are unique. There will never ever be another you.

- Do not compare yourself with others.

- Recognize and 'own' your talents and skills, and feel proud of who you are.

- Think about all the many, many things you have achieved in your life so far.

- Celebrate every success no matter how small.

- Be kind to yourself and look after yourself. Respect your body and look after it, and give yourself regular treats.

- Keep learning and trying things. The more you learn and achieve the better you feel about yourself.

- Help others; it's a great way of feeling good about yourself.

- Take a look at things that you feel are personal weaknesses and work on turning

EMOTIONAL INTELLIGENCE AND ENTERPRISE HANDBOOK
© CHERYL BUGGY (CONTINUUM 2008)

them a bit at a time, into strengths. However, remember nobody is perfect – in fact, who in their right mind would want to be!

 ## CURIOUS

- Find things that interest you, and learn all you can about those subjects or areas, and you will find your motivation grows. As that happens notice how your confidence grows as you become more knowledgeable.

- As well as exploring things that interest you, see if you can become curious about other related subjects and widen your knowledge.

- Learning and being curious also keeps boredom at bay, and makes you an interesting person to know.

- It also makes you very employable and, short of winning the lottery, we all need to work!

- The more curious you are about the world around you, the more ideas will pop into your head so you become more creative and enterprising.

- Once in a while try something you would never normally do or think you would be interested in, like buying a different magazine, watching something unusual on TV, going into a shop you have never visited before.

- Imagine you are an investigative journalist. Observe others carefully (without being rude!). Ask people questions. Remember the Who?, Why?, What?, When?, How? questions that journalists use and use them too.

# Top tips and memory joggers: how to be a winner

- Look after yourself. If you feed yourself junk food or junk thoughts you will get junk out! Respect your body.

- Spend time on an ongoing basis to get to know yourself. Having a good relationship with you is pretty important.

- Focus on the positive. Acknowledge and 'own' your good qualities and don't beat yourself up for what you are not. If you do want to change aspects of yourself get on and do it, don't feel sorry for yourself and just whinge and moan about it.

- Respect your feelings – all of them. If you are feeling down, nurture yourself (get help/support, etc.). If you are feeling good, try to hold on to that feeling for as long as you can.

- Help others whenever you can. It makes them feel special and it makes you feel good too.

- Celebrate every successful step and action you take, and help others celebrate too.

- Keep stress under control. Know what stresses you and have strategies and things you can do to reduce it.

- Face your fears; don't let them dominate your life.

- Avoid things or people that do not help you to thrive.

- Have a plan for your life with goals. You can always change the plan as you go along, but having one in the first place gives you momentum.

- Have the courage to take absolute responsibility for your life and be determined to have a great journey through it!

EMOTIONAL INTELLIGENCE AND ENTERPRISE HANDBOOK
© CHERYL BUGGY (CONTINUUM 2008)

## EMOTIONAL INTELLIGENCE AND ENTERPRISE ACTIVITIES AND CHALLENGES

The activities and challenges have been designed to encourage students to flex their EI and enterprise 'muscles'. Each one could cover a full half term, or they can be used to fill whatever time you have available. Either way, putting the EI and enterprise competencies into action is a sure way of helping embed them into the students' mindsets.

At the conclusion of any of the activities and challenges you could get the students to reflect on the competencies they have used/displayed, as well as listing which of them they have incorporated into their creations. Use the check list provided at the end of the sessions.

## Radio challenge

Divide the students into production teams of between four and six.

Each team has been given a two-hour speech and music show on their local radio station.

They need to select a topic or topics that are relevant to their age group. These can be personal, local, national or international in subject matter.

They then have to create a programme schedule, detailing:

- the title of the show
- subjects to be covered and why
- music to be played, what tracks and how long each track is
- guests to be interviewed
- questions to be asked
- how long each speech segment will last

They also have to write a 30-second commercial trailer for their programme.

The final step is to present back to the whole group their planned schedule and read out their commercial trailer.

As research the students might want to listen to the current formats of all their local stations and critique each one, paying particular attention to the speech content.

A variation on this challenge could be to get the class to come up with a new radio station concept and for each group to be responsible for parts of the station's output. For example, news, music, specific programmes, phone-ins, website, promotion, etc. They could then plan a 'bid' for a radio licence.

## EI changing rooms

Ask the students to put themselves into groups of four to six and give themselves a group name based on a colour, feeling, taste or smell.

The task is to design a room in the school or college that is to become a 'chill' space, a room where students can come to relax and de-stress.

They have to decide on the colour scheme and contents of the room to achieve the required effect.

Get them to research the impact of colours on moods, emotions and space via the internet or using the library. You might even consider inviting a colour consultant or interior designer in as a guest.

They also need to look at furniture and objects they might want to use in the room, for example an indoor water feature, paintings for the walls, bean bags, aromatherapy burner.

You might consider giving them a budget for this so that they have to produce a more structured business plan.

In the final session the groups will be required to present their ideas to the whole class. You might like to invite members of the senior management team or the headteacher to the presentation.

Students might also consider approaching local businesses with their idea, especially those in the DIY industries, in order to get them to sponsor the room and make it a reality.

## Stimulating open spaces

Put the students into groups of four to six, and get them to select a name for their group.

An outdoor space has been identified on the campus or nearby park which is to be used as an area for young children, aged between seven and eleven, where they can explore their imagination and creativity.

Ideas could include such things as a maze, sandpit, water feature, tree house, rubber construction blocks, wall for creating pictures or collages, mosaic squares, etc. The total space available is 15 metres square.

Each group needs to design the contents for this space and create a plan or model to put on display.

Beside each plan/model there needs to be a written explanation of the contents and the idea underpinning each one. For example, the construction blocks will allow children to become architects and design and build their own temporary fantasy space.

The display could be put up in the school foyer and other students could be encouraged to vote for the one they think is the most effective, or taken to local junior schools for feedback.

Students could be encouraged to make a pitch to their local council or to local businesses to see if their plan can become a reality.

## Web page for new arrivals into your year group

This can be an individual project or is suitable for groups of two to three.

The students have been given the design brief from a local junior school to design a section of a website that provides useful and positive information for students who are about to move up to secondary school.

They must decide on the page/s content and layout.

As they begin to plan, they might find the What?, Why?, How?, When?, Who? questions useful. For example, they might want to include: how to get from lesson to lesson by putting in a plan of the campus, who teaches what, how the school day is structured, where to go if you are worried, etc.

Once the planning has been completed the actual page/s can be created and when finished the whole group can vote for the one they think is the most effective and appropriate.

The winning creation could be offered to all the local junior schools who might like to add it to their own websites for the benefit of their pupils.

## Change the world on your doorstep – an environmental challenge

Divide the students into groups of four to six.

Give each group the responsibility of exploring one of the following environmental issues that are of concern in their neighbourhood, town or city, country and globally. For example, it could be about saving water, recycling paper, conserving power, reducing carbon footprints, etc.

They can research via the internet, for example, a Google search will bring up any number of agencies, organizations and groups who work in this field.

From their research they need to come up with five issues and from those select one that particularly concerns them and state why.

The next step is to come up with a campaign or action plan to raise awareness and create a response around their chosen theme.

They will then present their campaign plan back to the whole group, as well as create a poster for display around the campus, advertising their issue with a call to action or giving advice. For example, did you know that leaving the tap on while you brush your teeth would fill a swimming pool in a year? Turn it off while you brush!

To raise general awareness of being kind to the environment students could collect rubbish and make a collage or object for display. For example, make a dinosaur out of old computer and phone bits, cans, plastic, old paper and clothes.

## Fundraising challenge for the charity of your choice

Students can work in groups of two to six for this challenge.

The first step is for them to select a charity or not for profit organization that they want to support. If they have problems identifying one perhaps you might give them some suggestions or get them to explore possibilities in areas they are interested in, for example, children, the Third World, animals, etc., via the internet, library or local council.

They must then decide on how they are going to raise awareness and raise money and describe the event or action they want to take. This could be something they want to do e.g. a sponsored walk, car wash or fashion show, or to make e.g. tee shirts, cards or jewellery.

They need to plan a presentation to the rest of the group explaining:

- what charity they have chosen and why
- what their idea is
- how much money they aim to raise
- what their action plan is

The class could vote for the best idea, or you could invite charity representatives along to hear the presentations and give feedback.

The winning idea or all of the ideas could be actioned if time allows.


## Meaningful words

This activity can be done individually or in pairs.

Choosing either posters, commercials or the lyrics to a song as their medium, students have to create a message based on any of the six EI or six enterprise competencies.

After brainstorming planning, students should spend time turning their ideas into reality, and putting them on display or performing them.

## Dear ... agony aunt/uncle page

Use the six EI and six enterprise competencies as the basis for potential realistic problems that might be faced by students of their age. For example, feeling demotivated by coursework, scared to ask somebody out on a date.

Get the class to brainstorm ideas and issues, then in pairs get them to write a letter to an agony aunt/uncle, outlining a problem/situation based on one of the competencies e.g. empathy, courage, etc.

They then hand their 'problem' letter on to another pair who have to respond with suitable EI or enterprising advice.

Letters and responses can be shared with the whole group and discussed.

These can be posted up in the classroom, made into a magazine feature or put on a specially created web page.

## Magazine

This new class magazine has a teen target audience, and will need a name.

The class needs to vote for and appoint an overall editor, then brainstorm ideas for content. The focus must be on all or some of the EI and enterprise competencies. For example, a feature on clothes to wear to an interview, tips on how to boost your confidence, stories from successful role models, etc.

To help this process they could research magazines currently in the marketplace to get ideas about structure, style and formats, and what they like and dislike about what they see.

There then needs to be a division of labour and responsibilities with timelines for copy/articles to be completed. This is especially important if there are external interviews that need to take place (these of course can happen over the phone or by e-mail).

The editor needs to be responsible for making sure the team stick to their tasks and complete on time, and for proofreading the copy. He/she might want to appoint subeditors for this.

With any necessary help from the IT or other relevant

departments in the school or college, the prototype magazine can be printed off.

Some audience research would now be helpful for constructive feedback. They might also want to contact their local newspaper editor for feedback and advice or any local journalists. Or there is nothing wrong in approaching national magazines and asking for the same thing. Nothing ventured nothing gained! The completed product could then go on sale internally, although the students might want to see if they can attract an external audience too. There could also be an e-edition online.

## Take a shop – what would you do with it?

Allow the students to self-select into small groups.

They have been given an empty shop in their local shopping centre for one year. They have to decide how to use the shop for the benefit of their school/college and if possible their local community.

The benefits need to be both financial and also in terms of information and goodwill, so they will need to consider such things as fundraising ideas, communicating important messages and bringing people together.

Ideas might include: selling products they or people in their local community have made; telling the story of their school or college; sharing their hopes goals and dreams; allowing other relevant groups to share the space with them; inter-generational projects; displays about other cultures and religions to inform and take down barriers, etc.

They will have to make a case for their concept in an imaginative presentation to the class or at a school/college assembly. The best one could be voted for.

They will also have to design a quarter page advertisement for the local paper promoting the opening of the new shop.

In addition they must decide on the front window display of the shop for the opening and describe it either in words or in a diagram/drawing.

Finally, who would they invite to open the shop and why?

## Secrets of success

This activity requires students to set up, (with help if necessary) and carry out, interviews with successful people to explore their 'recipe' for success.

You could make use of the list of questions in the section on using guests.

The overall aim of the interviews is to see if there are common themes shared by successful people in terms of their use of the EI and enterprise competencies.

Get the class to brainstorm what list of questions they want to ask interviewees. Aim for six to ten questions that will reveal both the individual's story, and the competencies and qualities that they feel have helped them, or that they wish they had more of!

That list will form the blueprint so the same questions will be asked regardless of who is interviewing whom.

Decide who the interviews will be with, contact and set up the interviews. This can be face to face, via e-mail, telephone, or Skype, etc.

In drawing up a list of potential interviewees encourage the students to try for any famous or inspirational people that they admire. They might not succeed in getting an interview, but it's always worth a try. They might just get a positive response, especially if the response can be via e-mail or on the phone.

They could also look for people in their local community from the business sector, world of sport and entertainment, etc. There might also be some interesting past students who are now successful in their chosen career who would be happy to share their stories.

Get each interview written up (or, if you have the facility, recorded) and published in a booklet or put onto a CD so that the information can be used by other students.

## Marketing campaign for a new product

In self-selected groups of two to four ask the students to create a marketing campaign for a new product.

To begin with students might want to contact PR and marketing companies, either locally or via the internet, for some tips on what they need to be considering when they are putting a campaign together.

The product is a new chewing gum that has special proven qualities. When chewed, it improves your ability to learn and remember new information. It comes in three flavours – strawberry, mint and chocolate. It is low in calories, sugar free and not suitable for children under the age of eight.

Students must:

- Decide on the design of the wrapper including colour, lettering and product name.
- Create a commercial to promote the key qualities of the gum.
- Decide where and how to advertise the product and the target advice.
- Then each group is to present their 'pitch' back to the class.
- If they have made contact with a PR and marketing company, they might want to ask for feedback on their finished campaign.

## Time box

The class have been asked to select 10 to 12 items that will be placed in a box in the foundations of a new building in the neighbourhood. The items, (or photographs of the items if they are too big), need to reflect life today.

The students have to do two things:

- First, to do some research by questioning others in the school to explore what items they would choose. That research then needs to be collated to see if there is any common ground.
- Then, as a class, they need to make the final choices, with reasons for each choice.

It would be great to actually find an appropriate box and fill it with the chosen items and see if it can be buried in the foundations of any current local construction. Alternatively it could be buried somewhere on the school or college campus.

A variation of this activity would be to get each student to select items that reflect their life so far, along with symbols that represent what they want for their futures. Again they could each choose a box and fill it, keeping it safe to be explored and enjoyed in years to come.

## Alphabet game

In self-selected groups of not more than four, students have to design a game. It can be a visual, auditory, spoken or performing game (or all). It is aimed at five year olds and its intention is to teach them the alphabet.

Students need to brainstorm ideas, come up with a concept and present their ideas back to the class. They might want to try out their ideas with some infant school teachers or parents or five year olds.

Each group can than be given time to create their alphabet product and these can then be put on display. They could also explain whether what they have produced could actually be marketed and sold!

A variation on this would be to create a game for young children, that helps them learn how to be good friends, deal with fears or, alternatively how to be happy.

## Treasure hunt challenge

The aim of this challenge is to find a creative way of introducing new students to the school who are making their first visit from junior school.

Get the students into self-selected groups of about four.

The task is to design a treasure hunt experience that will take prospective students on a journey of discovery around the campus. In this way they will learn where the various subject departments are located, along with other key areas such as the sick room, reception, library and recreation areas.

The hunt should also encourage new students to find key members of staff and understand their roles and responsibilities.

Finally if the school has a set of rules or guidelines that students are expected to follow, these too should be added to the hunt.

Remind the groups that a treasure hunt consists of a series of clues that lead people step by step on a journey. At each step the participants are required to collect some information e.g. find the school crest in the reception area and copy the motto, or locate the main IT suite and count the number of computers, or locate the head of sports and find out how many different types of sport are played at the school.

Finished treasure hunts could be tried out by inviting a group of junior children in for their feedback.

A variation on this challenge could be to get the students to visit their local college or university and devise a treasure hunt for new students with the same aim and end result as above.

## New look design challenge

Get the students into self-selected mixed groups (male and female) of about four.

This challenge requires the groups to design a new look uniform or dress code for the senior years of their school.

They have to consider such things as:

- styles
- logos
- the seasons
- cost effectiveness
- colour and fabric
- accessories if required (e.g. bags, shoes, hats)

They may wish to do some online research into current fashions and trends, suppliers, etc., and to canvas the opinions of others in their year group.

They might also consider approaching fashion stores to borrow appropriate clothing for fashion show or to display on mannequins.

All groups need to mount a display of their choices, either just in their classroom, or elsewhere in the school for others to see and perhaps vote on.

## Deconstruct and reconstruct challenge

This activity aims to encourage creativity and stimulate curiosity by requiring students to take something apart and then create something entirely different.

Depending on the object, students need to be in groups of two to four.

This will also require them, with your guidance, to come up with a list of suitable objects to be taken apart and there needs to be team effort in locating them. Objects might include old clocks, mobile phones, computers, bicycles, watches, items of clothing.

Objects need to be disassembled with great care and delicacy – not to be attempted if you are at all worried about health and safety issues!

Encourage the students to explore and marvel at the cleverness of the construction, and get them to carefully lay out each piece in order.

See if they can attempt to reconstruct the object.

Then, get them to deconstruct once more and this time use the pieces and parts to create something entirely new and fantastical with a description of what the new object is and its purpose.

Put the finished items on display.

## Dream collages

For this activity you need a big pile of magazines and colour supplements.

Initially each student needs to think about the ingredients they would like to have for their lives. This needs to include such things as place to live, job to have, people, possessions, feelings, travel, leisure time, achievements, etc.

The next step is for them to go through the magazines and cut out pictures that represent these things. They then need to build a collage on a large piece of card. These can then be put on display, or if private, taken home. They serve as great memory joggers and inspire the students to move towards what they desire for their lives.

## Self-evaluation matrix

After each session, ask yourself which of the competencies you have found out about, or used, and give examples.

| The emotional intelligence competencies | How | What |
|---|---|---|
| Self-awareness | | |
| Self-responsibility | | |
| Positive & appreciative | | |
| Empathetic & respectful | | |
| Motivated | | |
| Persistent | | |

# Self-evaluation matrix

photocopiable

| The enterprise competencies | How | What |
|---|---|---|
| Using initiative | | |
| Dealing with uncertainty | | |
| Creative | | |
| Courageous | | |
| Confident | | |
| Curious | | |